Microsoft® Excel 2016

by Alex Scott, triOS College

LEVEL 1

LABYRINTH

LEARNING™

Microsoft Excel 2016: Level 1

Copyright © 2017 by Labyrinth Learning

LABYRINTH
LEARNING™

Labyrinth Learning
2560 9th Street, Suite 320
Berkeley, California 94710
800.522.9746
On the web at lablearning.com

Product Manager:
Jason Favro

Development Manager:
Laura Popelka

Senior Editor:
Alexandra Mummery

Junior Editor:
Alexandria Henderson

Assessment and Multimedia Content Development:
Ben Linford, Judy Mardar, Andrew Vaughnley

Production Manager:
Debra Grose

Compositor:
Happenstance Type-O-Rama

Indexer:
Valerie Perry

Interior Design:
Debra Grose

Cover Design:
Mick Koller

ebook only ITEM: 1-59136-848-0
          ISBN-13: 978-159136-848-9

ebook with printed textbook ITEM: 1-59136-849-9
                    ISBN-13: 978-159136-849-6

Manufactured in the United States of America

GPP 10 9 8 7 6 5 4 3

Table of Contents

Preface

This textbook is part of our brand-new approach to learning for introductory computer courses. We've kept the best elements of our proven instructional design and added powerful, interactive elements and assessments that offer enormous potential to engage learners in a new way. We're delighted with the results, and we hope that learners and educators are, too!

Why Did We Write This Content?

In today's digital world, knowing how to use the most common software applications is critical, and those who don't are left behind. Our goal is to simplify the entire learning experience and help every student develop the practical, real-world skills needed to be successful at work and in school. Using a combination of text, videos, interactive elements, and assessments, we begin with fundamental concepts and take learners through a systematic progression of exercises to reach mastery.

What Key Themes Did We Follow?

We had conversations with dozens of educators at community colleges, vocational schools, and other learning environments in preparation for this textbook. We listened and have adapted our learning solution to match the needs of a rapidly changing world, keeping the following common themes in mind:

Keep it about skills. Our content focus is on critical, job-ready topics and tasks, with a relentless focus on practical, real-world skills and common sense as well as step-by-step instruction to ensure that learners stay engaged from the first chapter forward. We've retained our proven method of progressively moving learners through increasingly independent exercises to ensure mastery—an approach that has been successfully developing skills for more than 20 years.

Keep it simple. Our integrated solutions create a seamless and engaging experience built on a uniquely dynamic instructional design that brings clarity to even the most challenging topics. We've focused our content on the things that matter most and have presented it in the easiest way for today's learners to absorb it. Concise chunks of text are combined with visually engaging and interactive elements to increase understanding for all types of learners.

Keep it relevant. Fresh, original, and constantly evolving content helps educators keep pace with today's student and work environments. We have reviewed every topic for relevancy and have updated it where needed to offer realistic examples and projects for learners.

How Do I Use This Book?

We understand that we are in a time of transition and that some students will still appreciate a print textbook to support their learning. Our comprehensive learning solution consists of a groundbreaking interactive ebook for primary content delivery and our easy-to-use eLab course management tool for assessment. We want to help students as they transition to a digital solution. Our interactive ebook contains learning content delivered in ways that will engage learners. Students can utilize a print text supplement in conjunction with the ebook that provides all the textual elements from the ebook in a full-color, spiral-bound print format.

Our eLab platform provides additional learning content such as overviews for each chapter, automatically graded projects and other assessments that accurately assess student skills, and clear feedback and analytics on student actions.

Included with Your Textbook Purchase

▸ *Interactive ebook*: A dynamic, engaging, and truly interactive textbook that includes elements such as videos, self-assessments, slide shows, and other interactive features. Highlighting, taking notes, and searching for content is easy.

▸ *eLab Course Management System*: A robust tool for accurate assessment, tracking of learner activity, and automated grading that includes a comprehensive set of instructor resources. eLab can be fully integrated with your LMS, making course management even easier.

▸ *Instructor resources*: This course is also supported on the Labyrinth website with a comprehensive instructor support package that includes detailed lesson plans, PowerPoint presentations, a course syllabus, test banks, additional exercises, and more.

▸ *Learning Resource Center*: The exercise files that accompany this textbook can be found within eLab and on the Learning Resource Center, which may be accessed from the ebook or online at **www.labyrinthelab.com/lrc**.

▸ *Overview chapter content*: The "Overview Chapter ISM" folder in the Instructor Support Materials package and the "Overview Chapter Files" folder in the Student Exercise File download include the helpful "Introducing Microsoft Office and Using Common Features" chapter. In addition to providing a discussion of the various Office versions, this chapter introduces a selection of features common throughout the Office applications. **We recommend that students complete this "overview" chapter first.**

We're excited to share this innovative, new approach with you, and we'd love you to share your experience with us at www.lablearning.com/share.

Display Settings

Multiple factors, including screen resolution, monitor size, and window size, can affect the appearance of the Microsoft Ribbon and its buttons. In this textbook, screen captures were taken at the native (recommended) screen resolutions in Office 2016 running Windows 10, with ClearType enabled.

Visual Conventions

This book uses visual and typographic cues to guide students through the lessons. Some of these cues are described below.

Cue Name	What It Does
`Type this text`	Text you type at the keyboard is printed in this typeface.
Action words	The important action words in exercise steps are presented in boldface.
Ribbon	Glossary terms are highlighted with a light yellow background.
Note! Tip! Warning!	Tips, notes, and warnings are called out with special icons.
⚠	Videos and WebSims that are a required part of this course are indicated by this icon.
Command→Command→ Command→Command	Commands to execute from the Ribbon are presented like this: Ribbon Tab→Command Group→Command→Subcommand.
≡ **Design→Themes→Themes** 🅰	These notes present shortcut steps for executing certain tasks.

Acknowledgements

Many individuals contribute to the development and completion of a textbook. This book has benefited significantly from the feedback and suggestions of the following reviewers:

Pam Silvers, *Asheville-Buncombe Technical Community College*

Ramiro Villareal, *Brookhaven College*

Teresa Loftis, *Inland Career Education Center*

Kim Pigeon, *Northeast Wisconsin Technical College*

Lynne Kemp, *North Country Community College*

Tom Martin, *Shasta College*

Karen LaPlant, *Hennepin Technical College*

Kay Gerken, *College of DuPage*

Colleen Kennedy, *Spokane Community College*

1

Tracking Customer Data

I n this chapter, you will use Excel to enter detailed information about customers into a worksheet. You will learn about fundamental Excel features as you create and modify a simple worksheet. By the end of the chapter, you will have a solid grasp of the basic tools used to create worksheets in Excel.

LEARNING OBJECTIVES

▸ Enter data into a worksheet

▸ Format a worksheet

▸ Apply number and date formats

▸ Enter a series of related data

▸ Perform simple calculations

▸ Create cell references and use cell references in formulas

▸ Print a worksheet

📂 Project: Tracking Customer Invoices

Airspace Travel is a company that provides luxurious travel packages to tropical destinations. It is a small, family-run business, and the owners want your help tracking their customer accounts using Excel. You will use Excel to calculate the total amount each customer owes for each trip.

Some of the important information to include for each customer is the airline, destination, number of guests, and cost per person.

Introducing Excel

Microsoft Excel is a very popular tool used by millions of people every day. Why do people like it? Partly because it makes work easier! Excel is a worksheet program that allows you to work with numbers and data much more quickly and efficiently than with the pen-and-paper method.

Excel can perform instant calculations and process, analyze, and store large amounts of data. It can perform a variety of tasks such as:

▶ Creating payment schedules and budgets

▶ Creating sales reports and performing analysis

▶ Tracking invoices and controlling inventory

▶ Creating databases or analyzing data imported from a database

The more you learn about and become skilled at using Excel, the more ways you will discover to make work fast and easy.

DEVELOP YOUR SKILLS: E1-D1

In this exercise, you will start Excel and open a blank workbook.

1. Click **Start**.
2. Type **Ex** and then choose **Excel 2016** from the list of suggestions.
3. Click the **Blank Workbook** template on the Excel Start screen.

   A new blank workbook appears.

 Always leave the file open at the end of an exercise unless instructed to close it.

What Is a Worksheet?

An Excel file is called a workbook, and it is comprised of one or more worksheets (also called spreadsheets), which can be used for small tasks or to create large databases of information. Each worksheet is made up of rows and columns of individual cells that contain data. When you open a new blank workbook, the selected cell is A1. Cell A1 is referred to this way because this is where column A meets row 1.

The selected cell, also known as the active cell, is indicated by the thick box around it. The active cell is where you can type data or insert objects into your worksheet.

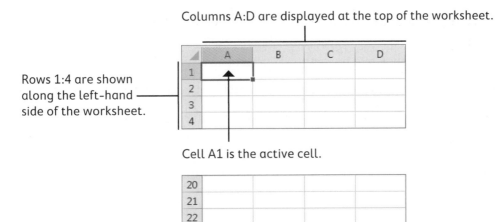

Columns A:D are displayed at the top of the worksheet.

Rows 1:4 are shown along the left-hand side of the worksheet.

Cell A1 is the active cell.

A new workbook has one worksheet, named *Sheet1* by default.

Cell Ranges

For many tasks, you want to select a group of cells instead of a single cell. A group of cells is referred to as a range. The cells in a range can be adjacent (side by side) or nonadjacent.

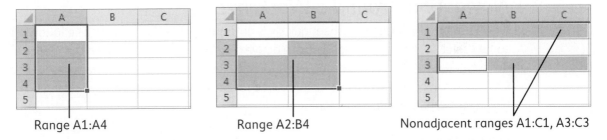

Range A1:A4

Range A2:B4

Nonadjacent ranges A1:C1, A3:C3

Entering and Editing Data

Data is easily entered into Excel by simply selecting a cell and typing. If a cell already contains data, you can double-click the cell to edit it. Text is used for headings or descriptive data, and numbers can either be typed into a cell or calculated with a formula.

Name Box—displays the name of the active cell (A1)

Formula Bar—displays the active cell entry

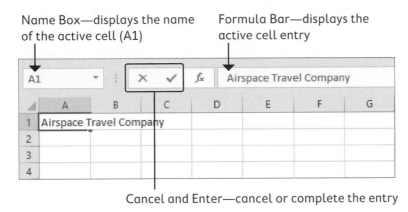

Cancel and Enter—cancel or complete the entry

Completing Cell Entries

After typing or editing data in a cell, you need to complete the entry before you can continue. The method you use to complete the entry will determine where the active cell moves.

Excel is in Ready mode when a cell is selected and Enter mode when data is being inserted. The difference between Enter and Ready modes is that many Excel features are unavailable while you are entering data.

Tapping `Enter`, `Tab`, or any of the arrow keys (`→`, `←`, `↑`, `↓`) will complete the entry as shown in the table below. Another option is to use the Enter `✓` button on the Formula Bar, which will keep the current cell active.

COMPLETING A CELL ENTRY

Completion Method	New Active Cell Location
`Enter`	Moves one cell down
`Tab`	Moves one cell to the right
`→`,`←`,`↑`,`↓`	Moves to the next cell in the direction of the arrow key
`✕`	Cancels the entry (or modification) and keeps the current cell active
`✓`	Completes the entry without moving

Navigating Around a Worksheet

Navigating around your worksheet quickly is an important skill to master. The following table lists some useful keystrokes for changing the active cell. You can also click with the mouse to select the desired cell or type a cell name into the Name Box to quickly jump to it. A worksheet has up to 1,048,576 rows and up to 16,384 columns, so for large amounts of data, you definitely want a quicker way to get around than simply scrolling!

NAVIGATION METHODS

Keystroke(s)	How the Active Cell Changes
`→`,`←`,`↑`,`↓`	One cell right, left, up, or down
`Home`	Beginning (column A) of current row
`Ctrl`+`Home`	Home cell, usually cell A1
`Ctrl`+`End`	Last cell in active part of worksheet
`Page Down`	Down one visible screen
`Page Up`	Up one visible screen
`Alt`+`Page Down`	One visible screen right
`Alt`+`Page Up`	One visible screen left
`Ctrl`+`G`	Displays Go To dialog box

In this exercise, you will enter the data for your worksheet title and headings.

Before You Begin: *Be sure to visit the Learning Resource Center at labyrinthelab.com/lrc to retrieve the exercise files for this course before beginning this exercise.*

1. Save your workbook as **E1-D2-Invoices** in your **Excel Chapter 1** folder.

2. Type **Airspace Travel Company** in **cell A1** and tap ⌊Enter⌋ to complete the entry.

   Notice that cell A2 is now the active cell.

3. Type **Monthly Customer Invoices** in **cell A2** and tap ⌊Enter⌋ to complete the entry.

   So far you've used the ⌊Enter⌋ key to move down column A while entering the data. Now you'll use the ⌊Tab⌋ key to move across row 3 as you enter more data.

4. Type **First Name** in **cell A3** and tap ⌊Tab⌋ to complete the entry and move one cell to the right.

5. Type **Last Name** in **cell B3** and tap ⌊Tab⌋.

   Notice the First Name text in cell A3 is no longer fully visible because it's wider than column A. Long entries are often cut off like this when the cell to their right contains data.

6. Type **Provider** in **cell C3** and tap ⌊Tab⌋.

7. Type **Destination** in **cell D3** and tap ⌊Tab⌋.

8. Type **# of Guests** in **cell E3**, but this time click Enter ☑ on the Formula Bar to complete the entry.

   Notice that cell E3 remains the active cell. Use Enter on the Formula Bar to complete entries when you want the current cell to remain active. Your worksheet should now look like this.

◢	A	B	C	D	E	F
1	Airspace Travel Company					
2	Monthly Customer Invoices					
3	First Nam	Last Name	Provider	Destinatio	# of Guests	

9. Save the workbook.

📖 Data Consistency in a Database

When inputting data, the consistency of the information is extremely important. If you are entering employee records in a large database, you want to ensure that information such as department names and position titles is entered accurately; for example, you wouldn't want some employees to be listed in the "Financial" department and others to be listed in the "Finance" department because that would create problems when looking up, sorting, and filtering your data.

Excel has a feature that helps with this problem and also saves a lot of time when you need to enter the same text repeatedly. AutoComplete will suggest text for you as you type, using data from the same column. For example, if you type "Accounting" for a department name in one cell and then farther down in the same column type the letter "A," AutoComplete will suggest "Accounting," and you can either accept the suggestion or ignore it and keep typing.

DEVELOP YOUR SKILLS: E1-D3

In this exercise, you will enter the customer data below each of the column headings.

1. Save your workbook as **E1-D3-Invoices**.

2. Click **cell A4** to select it and then enter the following data for Eric Snow in **row 4** using the ⎡Tab⎤ key to complete each entry:

3	First Name	Last Name	Provider	Destinatic	# of Guest
4	Eric	Snow	Sunwind	Jamaica	

3. Type **2** in **cell E4** and tap ⎡Enter⎤ to complete the entry.

   Notice the active cell moves to A5, the beginning of a new row. Excel presumes you are finished entering data in the row and wish to start a new row. This is one of Excel's built-in data entry features that make it faster to enter data into a worksheet or database. As long as you enter data using the ⎡Tab⎤ key continuously from left to right, the ⎡Enter⎤ key will bring you back to the first column of data to begin the next row. If the active cell does not move from E4 to A5, it is likely because you used the mouse to select a cell rather than the ⎡Tab⎤ key.

4. Type **Alison** in **cell A5**, **Lobosco** in **cell B5**, and type only the letter **S** in **cell C5**.

   Notice that Excel's AutoComplete feature prompts you with the name Sunwind.

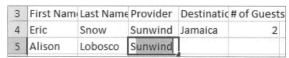

5. Tap the ⎡Tab⎤ key to accept the suggestion and continue entering the rest of the customer information in the following table, starting from **cell D5**.

   As you type the data, use ⎡Tab⎤ to accept the AutoComplete suggestions for Provider and Destination when possible; the goal is to enter the data quickly and efficiently. Remember to tap ⎡Enter⎤ at the end of each row to finish one customer's information and begin entering info for the next. Be aware that long entries won't fully display until the column is widened.

	A	B	C	D	E
3	First Name	Last Name	Provider	Destination	# of Guests
4	Eric	Snow	Sunwind	Jamaica	2
5	Alison	Lobosco	Sunwind	Mexico	2
6	Lacy	Henrich	TrueBlue	Dominican Republic	4
7	Will	Johns	Eastjet	Cuba	3
8	Nicki	Hollinger	Sunwind	Mexico	1
9	Lennard	Williams	TrueBlue	Brazil	6
10	Kerri	Knechtel	TrueBlue	Columbia	4
11	Karynn	Alida	Sunwind	Bahamas	2
12	David	Monton	Eastjet	Dominican Republic	2
13	Amanda	Campbell	Sunwind	Jamaica	7

6. Save the workbook.

Adjust Column Width and Row Height

To create enough space to properly see your text, you may need to adjust the column width and row height. A key step is to select the desired row(s) or column(s) before adjusting the size. Column width and row height can be set precisely using Ribbon commands or adjusted manually by dragging with the mouse. Even better, AutoFit can adjust the size to accommodate the largest entry in the column or row.

In a new workbook, column width is 8.43 and row height is 15.00; however, you might notice that cells are wider than they are tall. This is because column width is measured in characters and row height is measured in points, similar to font size. One character is bigger than one point.

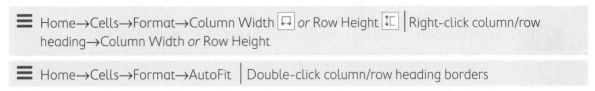

≡ Home→Cells→Format→Column Width ⟷ or Row Height ⇳ | Right-click column/row heading→Column Width or Row Height

≡ Home→Cells→Format→AutoFit | Double-click column/row heading borders

---

DEVELOP YOUR SKILLS: E1-D4

In this exercise, you will adjust the column widths using various methods in order to properly display the text in the cells.

1. Save your workbook as **E1-D4-Invoices**.
2. Follow these steps to manually adjust the width of column A:

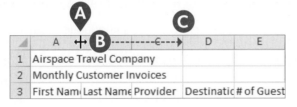

Ⓐ Move the mouse pointer over the line between the column A and B headings to display the Adjust pointer.

Ⓑ Press and hold the **left mouse button**, and notice the ScreenTip displays the current width of column A.

Ⓒ Continue holding the left mouse button and drag right until the text *First Name* is fully visible in cell A3. Release the mouse button.

As you drag, the column width is displayed as it changes. You can set column width to an exact amount this way, but it's difficult to be precise. You'll set precise widths later in this exercise.

3. Widen column B until *Last Name* is visible in **cell B3** or try to set the width to **10.00**.
4. Widen column C slightly or try to set the width to **10.00**.

Now you will ensure that columns A, B, and C are all set to exactly 10.00 using the Ribbon commands.

5. Follow these steps to select columns A:C:

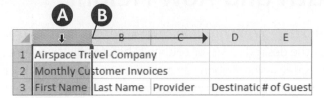

- **A** Position the mouse pointer on the column A heading and press and hold the **left mouse button**.
- **B** Drag right until **columns A:C** are selected and release the mouse button.

6. Choose **Home→Cells→Format→Column Width** ⟷ to display the Column Width box.

 You will see only a number in the box if all three columns have the same width.

7. If necessary, type the number **10** in the box and click **OK** to set the widths of columns A:C to 10.

8. Follow these steps to use AutoFit to adjust the width of column D:

- **A** Point between the column D and E headings to display the Adjust pointer.
- **B** Double-click to AutoFit column D. The width of column D will adjust to fit the widest entry.

Column D should now be wide enough so the text Dominican Republic *is fully visible in cells D6 and D12.*

9. Save the workbook.

Formatting Cells

You may notice that unformatted data does not look very pleasing. The columns are too narrow, and the black-and-white color is very plain and boring. Formatting is important not simply to make worksheets more appealing, but also to make it easier to read and interpret the data they contain. A textbook would be very hard to read if all the text was the same font and size, with all text the same color on a white page. Likewise, it is much easier to understand a worksheet if it is properly formatted.

Borders and Fill

Adding some color to your worksheet can accentuate the column headings and helps the data stand out. In addition to changing the font, style, and color of the text, you can use Fill Color to add color or shading inside a cell and use Borders to add lines around the cells. The drop-down menu buttons (▼) give you more choices for lines and colors.

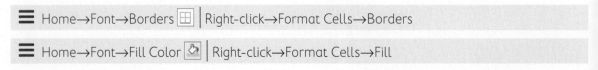

≡ Home→Font→Borders ⊞ | Right-click→Format Cells→Borders

≡ Home→Font→Fill Color 🖎 | Right-click→Format Cells→Fill

In this exercise, you will add some color to your worksheet using Fill Color, Borders, and Font Color.

1. Save your workbook as **E1-D5-Invoices**.

2. Follow these steps to select the column headings in the **range A3:E3**:

  Ⓐ Point to the middle of **cell A3** and press and hold down the **left mouse button**.

  Ⓑ Continue to hold the left mouse button as you drag right, along row 3, until the **range A3:E3** is selected.

  Ⓒ Release the mouse button to complete the selection.

3. Follow these steps to explore the Fill Color palette and apply a color:

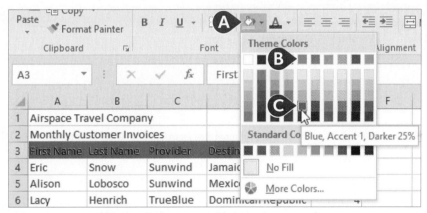

  Ⓐ Click the **Fill Color menu** button ▼ to display the palette.

  Ⓑ Notice the ScreenTip tells you the name of the color as you mouse over each one. The top row under Theme Colors gives you 10 options, with different shades for each color listed in the column below.

  Ⓒ Choose **Blue, Accent 1, Darker 25%** (fifth column, fifth row).

4. With the **range A3:E3** still selected, choose **Home→Font→Border** ⊞ **menu button** ▼.

5. Choose **Thick Outside Borders** to apply a thick border around the selected range.

6. For the same range choose **Home→Font→Font Color** 🅰 **menu button** ▼ and choose **White, Background 1** (first column, first row).

7. Then use the keyboard shortcut ⌑Ctrl⌑+⌑B⌑ to apply **Bold** format.

   Now that you have modified the headings, it's time to work on the titles.

8. Select **cell A1** and increase the Font Size to **18**, select **cell A2**, and increase the Font Size to **14**.

9. Next select the **range A1:A2**, apply the Font Color **Blue, Accent 1, Darker 50%** (fifth column, sixth row), and apply **Bold** ⌑B⌑ format.

10. Select the **range A4:B13** and apply **Bold** ⌑B⌑.

EXCEL

11. Click anywhere outside your data to deselect it; then, save the file. Your worksheet should now look like this.

▲	A	B	C	D	E
1	**Airspace Travel Company**				
2	**Monthly Customer Invoices**				
3	First Name	Last Name	Provider	Destination	# of Guest
4	Eric	Snow	Sunwind	Jamaica	2
5	Alison	Lobosco	Sunwind	Mexico	2

12. Save the workbook.

Cell Alignment

Excel's alignment tools let you adjust the arrangement of entries within cells. The default alignment for text data is left-aligned inside the cell, and the default for numerical data is right-aligned, as seen in column E in the previous exercise. The Alignment group on the Home tab provides you with the following options.

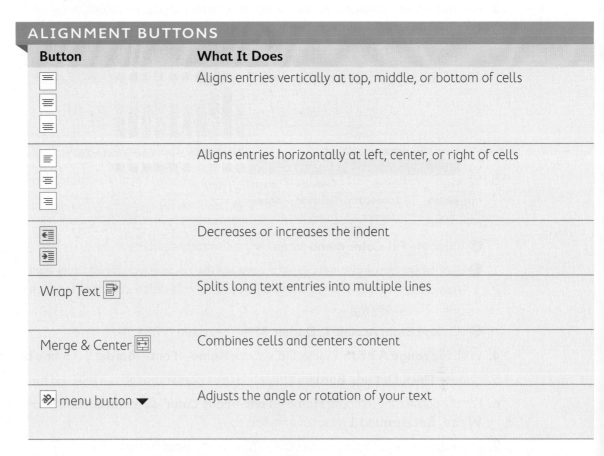

ALIGNMENT BUTTONS

Button	What It Does
	Aligns entries vertically at top, middle, or bottom of cells
	Aligns entries horizontally at left, center, or right of cells
	Decreases or increases the indent
Wrap Text	Splits long text entries into multiple lines
Merge & Center	Combines cells and centers content
menu button ▼	Adjusts the angle or rotation of your text

Merge & Center is a one-step method for simultaneously merging multiple cells into one cell and centering the content. This is often used for worksheet titles at the top of your sheet. You can also add an indent to the contents of a cell, which increases the distance of the text from the cell border. This adds more space, making it easier to read the data.

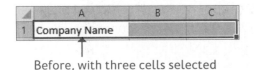

Before, with three cells selected

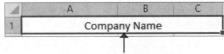

After applying Merge & Center,
one cell spans the three columns.

≡ Home→Alignment | Right-click→ Format Cells→ Alignment

Clear Formatting and Clear All

Occasionally you may want to keep text in a cell or range but clear all formatting, and you can do this by using the Clear Formatting feature. You can also remove text and formatting at the same time with Clear All.

≡ Home→Editing→Clear

DEVELOP YOUR SKILLS: E1-D6

In this exercise, you will adjust the alignment for your headings and data and use Merge & Center for your titles.

1. Save your workbook as **E1-D6-Invoices**.
2. Select the **range A3:E3** and choose **Home→Alignment→Wrap Text** 📃.

   Wrap Text takes a long entry and splits it into multiple lines, increasing row height at the same time.
3. With the **range A3:E3** still selected, choose **Home→Alignment→Middle Align** ≡.
4. With the headings still selected, choose **Home→Alignment→Center** ≡.
5. Select the **range E4:E13** (the number of guests data) and apply **Center** alignment ≡.
6. In the top row, select the **range A1:E1**.
7. Choose **Home→Alignment→Merge & Center** ⊞ (do not click the menu button ▼) to center the company name over the data below.
8. **Merge & Center** ⊞ the **range A2:E2** in the second row to center the Monthly Customer Invoices title as well.
9. Select the **range A4:A13** and choose **Home→Alignment→Increase Indent** 📑.
10. Save the workbook.

Working with Numbers and Dates

Because Excel is often used to perform calculations, it is important to understand how to enter numerical data properly. A number that is entered into Excel can be formatted many ways—with a dollar sign, percent symbol, decimals, or no decimals—but the numerical entry in the cell does not change. Typically to enter a numerical value into a cell, you want to simply type in the digits and adjust formatting after.

The default Number Format is General, which has no specific format. When a number format is applied to a cell, it remains with the cell even if the contents are changed or deleted. The table below provides some basic number format examples.

Number	Format	Result
2317.25	General	2317.25
2317.25	Comma Style	2,317.25
2317.25	Currency	$2,317.25
2317.25	Accounting	$ 2,317.25
0.25	Percent	25%

 Notice the differences between Currency and Accounting are the position of the $ sign and the indent from the right side of the cell.

The Number Format for the current cell is visible in the Number Format box.

Number format box

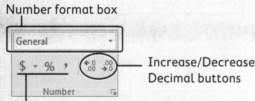

Increase/Decrease Decimal buttons

Format buttons for Accounting, Percent, and Comma Styles

Be aware that the numerical entry in the cell does not change when you increase or decrease the decimal (or when you change the Number Format). Doing so changes only the *appearance* of that number. Numbers with decimals can still have the decimals removed (decreased), but the number would then appear rounded up or rounded down from the actual entry, as shown in the table below. If the cell were used in a formula, the formula would still use the actual numerical entry in the cell, not the rounded version displayed on the screen.

Number	Decimal Places	Result	
23.64	3	23.640	Extra zero
23.64	2	23.64	No change
23.64	1	23.6	Rounded down
23.64	0	24	Rounded up

☰ Home→Number | Right-click→Format Cells→Number

Negative Numbers

Working with negative numbers is no different from other numbers, except that there are more options for displaying the negative values. Negative numbers have the currency, comma, and decimal options, but they can also be represented by a – (minus) symbol, red digits, brackets, or both red digits and brackets.

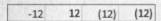

Formatting examples for negative twelve

Date Entries

Date formatting is another kind of number formatting. After a cell has a date entered into it, you can change the display without changing the actual cell entry. Excel can also use dates to perform calculations in a formula.

Dates can be entered many ways. However, the best way is to enter it in the format MM/DD for the current year or MM/DD/YY for any other year. For example, 10/15 would be entered for Oct. 15 of this year, and 10/15/14 would be entered for Oct. 15, 2014.

DEVELOP YOUR SKILLS: E1-D7

In this exercise, you will enter two new columns of information using currency and date formatting.

1. Save your workbook as **E1-D7-Invoices**.

2. Select **cell F3**, enter the heading **Price Per Person**, and then tap Tab .

   Notice the Font, Fill, and Wrap Text formatting are copied from the previous headings but the Border is not.

3. Enter the heading **Invoice Date** in **cell G3**.

4. Select the **range F3:G3** and apply the **Thick Outside Border**.

5. Select **cell F4**, type the digits **899**, and then tap Tab .

6. In **cell G4** type **9/8** and then click **Enter** on the Formula Bar.

   *Notice the digits **9/8** are automatically converted to display 8-Sep instead. In the Home→Number→Number Format box you can see the number format for cell G4 has changed to a Custom format.*

7. Continue entering the following data in columns F and G, respectively, starting in **cell F5**.

   The Number Format of the Invoice Date column is adjusted for you as you enter the data, as it was in cell G4. You will adjust the Number Format for the Price Per Person column after you have entered all the data.

	F	G
5	770	9/7
6	1200	9/1
7	950	9/9
8	875	9/8
9	800	9/8
10	560	9/5
11	870	9/8
12	650	9/6
13	900	9/9

8. In column F, select the range **range F4:F13** (the cells with the prices you just entered).

9. Choose **Home→Number→Accounting** $ (not the menu button ▼) to apply the Accounting format to the selection.

   The prices now have a dollar sign, comma separator, and two decimal places. All of the prices are even dollar amounts, so you can now eliminate the unnecessary decimals.

10. With the **range F4:F13** still selected, click **Home→Number→Decrease Decimal** twice.

11. Save the workbook.

Enter a Series Using AutoFill

When entering data into a worksheet, it is common to enter a series of data, which is a sequence of text, numbers, or dates. Rather than type each item line by line, you can use AutoFill to quickly enter an entire column of data. To use AutoFill, you can either drag the fill handle or double-click the fill handle.

The fill handle

After you use AutoFill, the AutoFill Options appear below the filled cells. AutoFill Options allow you to modify the way the data was filled, and the options change depending on the type of data that was filled. For example, filling in a series of dates allows you to choose days, weekdays, months, or years.

View the video "Using AutoFill to Fill a Series."

View the video "Using AutoFill Options."

DEVELOP YOUR SKILLS: E1-D8

In this exercise, you will enter the Invoice numbers for each customer using AutoFill.

1. Save your workbook as **E1-D8-Invoices**.
2. Type the column heading **Invoice #** in **cell H3** and then tap Enter.
3. In **cell H4** type **#3982** and then click Enter ☑ on the Formula Bar so that cell H4 remains active.

   The Invoice number for Eric's trip is #3982. The Invoice numbers will continue in sequence counting up by one, so the next Invoice will be #3983 and so on.

4. Follow these steps to use AutoFill to enter the rest of the invoice numbers:

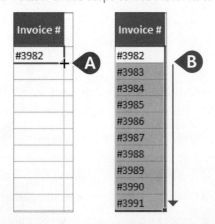

  Ⓐ In the active cell, place the mouse over the fill handle so that your pointer changes to the black cross.

  Ⓑ Drag down to **cell H13** to fill in the rest of the series.

   The Invoice numbers have now been entered for all customers, ending with #3991 in cell H13.

5. Save the workbook.

Perform Worksheet Calculations

Excel uses formulas to perform calculations, which are written as mathematical problems. To create a formula, you should always begin by typing the **=** sign in the cell. Then you list the numbers or cells to use in the formula, along with the operation to be performed.

The Formula Bar always displays the formula, but the cell displays the results.

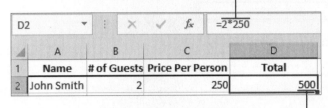

The formula =2*250 is entered in cell D2 and is displayed in the Formula Bar.

The result of the formula, 500, is displayed in cell D2.

Mathematical Operators

Common operations include addition, subtraction, multiplication, and division. The following table shows the corresponding keystroke for each operation.

Operation	Keystroke
Addition	+
Subtraction	–
Multiplication	*
Division	/

BEDMAS

When there is more than one operation in a formula, Excel must decide which operation to perform first. Excel follows the standard order of operations, commonly remembered by the acronym BEDMAS. That is, *Brackets first (also called parentheses), then Exponents, Division, Multiplication, Addition, and Subtraction.*

In Excel, you type formulas with rounded brackets/parentheses ( ) and not square brackets [ ]. For this reason the BEDMAS rule is also known as the PEMDAS rule, which is often remembered with the phrase "Please Excuse My Dear Aunt Sally."

It's important to understand the order of operations because it can significantly change the outcome of your formula. The formula =2+3*5 would result in 17 because 3*5 is the first operation and then 2+15 is 17. The formula =(2+3)*5 on the other hand results in 25, because (2+3) is the first operation and then 5*5 is 25.

 View the video "Using Simple Formulas."

 View the video "Understanding the BEDMAS Rule."

Cell References

Rather than typing numbers into your formulas, it is a good idea to use cell references whenever possible. A cell reference takes the place of a number in a formula and makes it easier to copy formulas down a column or across a row. So instead of =2*250, you could use =B2*C2 with the value 2 in cell B2, and the value 250 in cell C2.

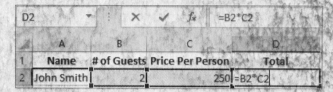

The formula in **cell D2** references **cells B2** and **C2**.

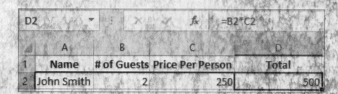

The formula result is 500.

Cell references can be typed, using upper- or lowercase letters, or you can simply click with the mouse on the cell you want to use.

Another advantage of cell references is that Excel automatically recalculates the formula if the value in the cell reference changes. In the example above, if the value in **cell C2** is changed to *350*, the formula in **cell D2** is automatically updated to show the new result, *700*, without any effort required.

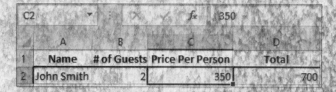

The formula result in **cell D2** is updated immediately when **cell C2** is changed.

DEVELOP YOUR SKILLS: E1-D9

In this exercise, you will add a column with a formula to calculate the subtotal for each customer.

1. Save your workbook as **E1-D9-Invoices**.

2. Select **cell I3**, type **Subtotal**, and then tap [Enter].

3. In **cell I4** type **=E4*F4** and then tap [Enter].

   Notice that as you type each cell reference, it adds a color to both the cell reference and the cell being referenced. The text E4 turns blue, and the cell will have a border and light shading of the same color around it. Then as you continue typing the formula, the text F4 turns red. The color changes each time you add a new cell reference, which helps you visualize the cell references while entering or editing the formula.

   You entered the formula that multiplied the # of Guests by the Price Per Person, and cell I4 should now show the result as $1,798. Now you will enter the next formula using the mouse instead of typing the cell references.

4. In **cell I5** type **=**, click **cell E5** to select it, type ***** and click **cell F5** to select it, and then click **Enter** ✓.

   The formula is similar, but this time the cell references refer to the information in row 5, and the result is $1,540. Notice that the formula in cell I4 uses cell references to cells E4 and F4, and cell I5 refers to cells E5 and F5, which means the relative position is the same. This means you can copy the formula down the column using AutoFill, rather than typing it in each time.

5. Point to the fill handle in **cell I5** and drag down to **cell I13**.

   The subtotal is now calculated for all customers. The subtotal column has copied the number format from column F; however, you will adjust it now to show two decimals.

6. Select the **range I4:I13** and click **Home→Number→Increase Decimal** ⬚ twice.

   Next you will add a new column to calculate the tax on each Subtotal. The tax rate is 8%.

7. Select **cell J3**, type **Tax**, and then tap ⬚Enter⬚.

8. In **cell J4** type **=**, click **cell I4** to select it, type ***8%**, and click **Enter** ✓.

   The tax has been calculated for the first customer as $143.84. Now you can copy the formula down for the rest of the column.

9. Point to the fill handle in **cell J4**, and this time double-click the fill handle.

   Double-clicking automatically fills the cells down the column according to the rows used in adjacent columns. The tax has been entered for all customers, so the last step is to calculate the Total by adding the Tax to the Subtotal.

10. Select **cell K3**, type **Total**, and then tap ⬚Enter⬚.

11. In **cell K4** type **=I4+J4** and click **Enter** ✓.

12. Point to the fill handle in **cell K4** and double-click to fill the Tax formula down Column K.

    All of the data has been entered, and now your formulas calculate the total owing for each customer. Your worksheet now looks like this.

	A	B	C	D	E	F	G	H	I	J	K
1			Airspace Travel Company								
2			Monthly Customer Invoices								
3	First Name	Last Name	Provider	Destination	# of Guests	Price Per Person	Invoice Date	Invoice #	Subtotal	Tax	Total
4	Eric	Snow	Sunwind	Jamaica	2	$ 899	8-Sep	#3982	$1,798.00	$143.84	$1,941.84
5	Alison	Lobosco	Sunwind	Mexico	2	$ 770	7-Sep	#3983	$1,540.00	$123.20	$1,663.20
6	Lacy	Henrich	TrueBlue	Dominican Republic	4	$ 1,200	1-Sep	#3984	$4,800.00	$384.00	$5,184.00
7	Will	Johns	Eastjet	Cuba	3	$ 950	9-Sep	#3985	$2,850.00	$228.00	$3,078.00
8	Nicki	Hollinger	Sunwind	Mexico	1	$ 875	8-Sep	#3986	$ 875.00	$ 70.00	$ 945.00
9	Lennard	Williams	TrueBlue	Brazil	6	$ 800	8-Sep	#3987	$4,800.00	$384.00	$5,184.00
10	Kerri	Knechtel	TrueBlue	Columbia	4	$ 560	5-Sep	#3988	$2,240.00	$179.20	$2,419.20
11	Karynn	Alida	Sunwind	Bahamas	2	$ 870	8-Sep	#3989	$1,740.00	$139.20	$1,879.20
12	David	Monton	Eastjet	Dominican Republic	2	$ 650	6-Sep	#3990	$1,300.00	$104.00	$1,404.00
13	Amanda	Campbell	Sunwind	Jamaica	7	$ 900	9-Sep	#3991	$6,300.00	$504.00	$6,804.00

13. Save the workbook.

Print a Worksheet

Now that the worksheet has all of the required information entered, you may want to print your data. Although printing is becoming less common in the digital age, occasionally you still need a paper copy. Printing a worksheet is simple, although sometimes adjustments need to be made so the cells, columns, and rows fit on a page nicely.

It is important to understand that printing in Excel prints the contents of the cells as displayed on the screen, not the formulas in the Formula Bar.

To adjust the way your worksheet prints, you can use the Scale to Fit feature. This will automatically resize your content to print the desired number of pages.

Excel will normally not print the gridlines around the cells or the row and column headings. However, if you wanted to print either Gridlines or Headings, you would simply check off these boxes in Sheet Options.

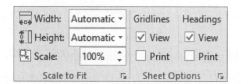

Because Excel can contain multiple worksheets, there are three options for printing. You can print the active worksheet, which is the default option, you can print the whole workbook, or you can print only the selected cells.

≡ File→Print→Settings

≡ Page Layout→Scale to Fit

≡ Page Layout→Sheet Options

DEVELOP YOUR SKILLS: E1-D10

In this exercise, you will begin with some formatting adjustments to put the finishing touches on your worksheet, access the print preview, and prepare your worksheet to be printed.

1. Save your worksheet as **E1-D10-Invoices**.
2. Select the **range K4:K13** (customer totals) and choose **Bold** B .

   If your digits are replaced with number signs (######), then it means your columns aren't wide enough to display the number; widen the columns as necessary.
3. Select the **range A3:K3** and choose **Home→Font→Border** ⊞ **menu button ▼→No Border**.

   This removes all of the borders from the column headings so that you can reapply the border around all headings.
4. With the **range A3:K3** still selected, choose **Home→Font→Border** ⊞ **menu button ▼→ Thick Outside Borders**.

   Now you need to center the titles over the data, including the newly added columns.

5. In the top row select the **range A1:K1** and click **Home→Alignment→Merge & Center** twice.

   The first time you click Merge & Center removes it from the first five columns, and the second time reapplies the Merge & Center across all eleven columns.

6. In row 2 select the **range A2:K2** and again click **Home→Alignment→Merge & Center** twice.

   Both titles should now be centered over your data.

Change Print Options

7. Choose **File→Print** to access the Print Preview.

   Notice the document will print on two pages, with the Invoice # column appearing at the right side of page one. You will also notice that the gridlines, which are the lines around the cells on the worksheet, do not print, nor do the Row or Column Headings. Now you will adjust the document to print only on one page.

8. Click **Back** to return to your worksheet.

   You will now see a dashed line between column H and column I, which indicates the Print Area for your worksheet.

9. Choose **Page Layout→Scale to Fit→ Width: Automatic** **menu button ▼→1 page**.

   The vertical dashed line is removed because the worksheet now prints one page-width only. The Scale is automatically adjusted and cannot be changed.

   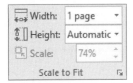

   Now you will select an area of the sheet to print.

10. Select the **range A1:K8** (the titles, headings, and data for the first five customers) and then choose **File→Print** to access Print Preview again.

    You can see in the preview the file will now print on one page.

11. Below Settings choose **Print Active Sheets→Print Selection**.

    The print preview changes to show that the print area will include only the first five customers now. There is a lot of white space on the bottom, so we can adjust the Orientation of the page as well.

12. Below Settings choose **Portrait Orientation→Landscape Orientation**.

    The printout will be much easier to read now with page turned to Landscape. Do not print at this time.

13. Save the workbook and close Excel.

Self-Assessment

 Check your knowledge of this chapter's key concepts and skills using the Self-Assessment in your ebook or eLab course.

Reinforce Your Skills

Enter Data and Format a Worksheet

Kids for Change is a nonprofit organization that helps minors participate and organize community service, fundraisers, and social events. In this exercise, you will create a worksheet that will allow Kids for Change to list the items required for purchase for an upcoming charity event.

1. Start Excel, open a new Blank Workbook, and save it in your **Excel Chapter 1** folder as **E1-R1-Purchases**.

Enter Data

2. In **cell A1** type **Kids for Change** and then tap [Enter].
3. In **cell A2** type **Items for Purchase** and then tap [Enter].
4. In **row 3** enter the following headings across the **range A3:D3**:

3	Item Name	Order By	Quantity	Price

5. In **rows 4:8** enter the following items for purchase:

4	T-shirts	5/12/2015	200	12.99
5	Buttons	5/20/2015	100	6.5
6	Hamburgers	5/30/2015	45	9.29
7	Buns	5/30/2015	45	2.19
8	Water	5/30/2015	12	1.99

Format the Worksheet

6. Select **column A**, choose **Home→Cells→Format→Column Width**, type **12**, and then tap [Enter].
7. Select the **range A1:A2** and then choose **Home→Font→Font Color** [A] menu button ▼→**Standard Purple**.
8. With the titles still selected, click **Home→Font→Increase Font Size** [A] two times so it is set to 14 points and then press [Ctrl]+[B] to apply Bold format.
9. Select the **range A3:D3** and then choose **Home→Font→Fill Color** [⬧] menu button ▼→**Blue, Accent 5, Lighter 60%** (ninth column, third row).
10. With the same range selected, apply the same **Standard Purple** font color and **Bold** formatting.
11. With the headings still selected, choose **Home→Alignment→Center** [≡] to center the headings.
12. Select the **range B4:B8** and choose **Home→Number→Number Format→Long Date**.

    The day of the week is important, so now you can see the day displayed in the cells.

13. Select the **range D4:D8** and apply the **Accounting Number** format.
14. Save the workbook.

Fill a Series and Use Formulas

In this exercise, you will find the total that Kids for Change needs to spend on supplies for each purchase and fill in purchase order numbers using a series.

1. Save your workbook as **E1-R2-Purchases**.
2. Select **cell E3**, enter the heading **Subtotal**, and then tap Enter.
3. In **cell E4** enter the formula **=C4*D4** and click **Enter** ✓ on the Formula Bar.
4. Double-click the fill handle in **cell E4** to fill the formula down the column.

   As a charity, Kids for Change qualifies for a discount, so you will now calculate a 15% discount on all purchases.

5. Select **cell F3**, type the heading **Discount**, and then tap Tab.
6. In **cell G3** type the heading **Total** and then tap Enter.
7. In **cell F4** enter the formula **=E4*15%** and then tap Tab.
8. In **cell G4** enter the formula **=E4-F4** and then tap Enter.
9. Select the **range F4:G4**, which contains the two formulas you just entered, and fill both formulas down **column F** and **column G** to **row 8**.
10. Select **cell H3**, enter the heading **Purchase #**, and then tap Enter.
11. In **cell H4** type **#335** and click **Enter** ✓.
12. Use the fill handle in **cell H4** to fill the series of Purchase #s down the column.
13. Adjust the width of **column H** using AutoFit so the column heading is fully visible.
14. Select the **range H4:H8** and change the cell alignment to **Align Right**.
15. Go to the Print Preview and under Settings adjust the page orientation to **Landscape** but do not print at this time.
16. Save the workbook and close Excel.

Create and Format a Worksheet with Formulas

In this exercise, you will help Kids for Change calculate the funds raised during one of its charity events.

1. Start Excel, open a new Blank Workbook, and save it in your **Excel Chapter 1** folder as **E1-R3-Pledges**.

2. Beginning in **cell A1**, enter the following data:

	A	B	C	D
1	Kids for Change			
2	Summer Charity Race			
3	Participant	Sign-up Date	Pledges	Miles Run
4	Shelly Mundt	4/23	5	25
5	Pauline Alvarado	4/25	12	15
6	Chris Driedger	4/2	14	10
7	Korey Rhynold	3/29	19	15
8	Kimberly Ayres	4/17	23	5
9	Glenn Edwards	4/3	17	25
10	Inga Maier	4/12	12	10

3. Use **AutoFit** to resize **columns A** and **B**.

4. In **cell E3** enter the heading **Bib #** and tap Enter.

5. In **cell E4** type **KCSCR410** and then use **AutoFill** to complete the series of Bib #s.

6. In **cell F3** enter the heading **Total Raised**.

   Each participant gathers pledges from donors, and each pledge will donate $1 for each mile run, so we can calculate the total each participant raised by multiplying Pledges x Miles Run.

7. In **cell F4** enter the formula **=C4*D4**.

8. Use **AutoFill** to copy the formula down for the other participants.

9. With the total raised in the **range F4:F10** still selected, apply the **Currency** number format.

10. Resize **column F** to make it wide enough to fit the column heading.

11. Select the **range B4:B10** and apply the **Short Date** format.

12. Select the **range C4:D10** (the data for Pledges and Miles Run) and center-align the data.

13. Select the **range A1:F1** and apply **Merge & Center**.

14. Select the **range A2:F2** and apply **Merge & Center**.

15. Select the **range A1:F3** (titles and headings) and apply the Fill Color **Standard Dark Blue**.

16. With the same range selected, apply the Font Color **White, Background 1**.

17. Save the workbook and close Excel.

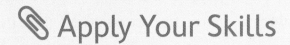

Apply Your Skills

Enter Data and Format a Worksheet

Universal Corporate Events is a meeting and event planning service, which hosts and organizes company meetings, retreats, and parties. In this exercise, Universal Corporate Events would like you to prepare a spreadsheet to compare available office space for a second office.

1. Start Excel, open a new Blank Workbook, and save it in your **Excel Chapter 1** folder as **E1-A1-Listings**.

2. Beginning in **cell A1**, enter the following data:

	A	B	C	D	E
1	Universal Corporate Events				
2	Potential Office Space				
3	Address	Building Class	List Date	Square Ft	Monthly Rent
4	3100 Sycamore Lane	A	7/21	1200	2500
5	1812 Broadway	A	3/17	1050	2250
6	21 King Street	B	5/22	1450	1875
7	6801 Delamere Way	C	7/16	1700	2150
8	48 Franklin Blvd.	B	5/30	920	1500

3. Select the **range A3:E3** and apply **Wrap Text** format.

4. With the headings still selected, apply **Middle Align** and **Center**.

5. Adjust the column width for **column A** to exactly **18.00**.

6. Select the **range B4:B8** and apply the **Center** alignment.

7. Select the **range E4:E8** and apply **Accounting Number Format**. Then remove both decimal places.

8. Select **cell A1** and increase the font size to **18**.

9. Select **cell A2** and increase the font size to **14**.

10. Select the **range A3:E3** and increase the font size to **12**.

11. With the headings still selected, apply the Fill Color **Gold, Accent 4**.

12. Select the **range A1:E3** and apply **Bold** format.

13. Save the workbook.

Use Formulas with Cell References

In this exercise, you will create formulas to calculate additional information that Universal Corporate Events can use to make a decision about office space.

1. Save your workbook as **E1-A2-Listings**.

2. In **cell F3** enter the heading **Price per SqFt**.

3. In **cell F4** enter the formula **=E4/D4** and then fill the formula down the rest of the column.

4. In **cell G3** enter the heading **Maint. Fees**.

5. Fees are 4% of the monthly rent, so in **cell G4** enter a formula to calculate the fees. (Hint: The result in **cell G4** should be *$100*.)

6. Fill the formula in **cell G4** down the column for the other listings.

7. In **cell H3** enter the heading `Annual Cost`.

8. In **cell H4** enter the formula for annual cost, which will add monthly rent plus maintenance fees, and then multiply by 12. (Hint: Remember BEDMAS, and use brackets to perform the addition first. The result in cell H4 should be *31200*.)

9. With **cell H4** selected, apply the **Accounting Number Format** and remove both decimal places.

10. Apply **Bold** format to **cell H4** and then fill the formula in **cell H4** down the column.

11. Select the **range A3:H3** and apply a **Top** and **Bottom** Border.

12. Save the workbook and close Excel.

APPLY YOUR SKILLS: E1-A3

Create a Financial Report

In this exercise, you will enter data for clients who have booked events and use formulas to calculate how much they still owe.

1. Start Excel, open a new Blank Workbook, and save it in your **Excel Chapter 1** folder as `E1-A3-Income`.

2. Beginning in **cell A1**, enter the following data:

	A	B	C	D
1	Universal Corporate Events			
2	June Income Forecast			
3	Client	Event	Event Date	Fee
4	Green Clean	Staff Party	6/13	480
5	Kids for Change	Training	6/18	325
6	Blue Jean Landscaping	Training	6/14	550
7	Stormy BBQ	Team Building	6/23	750
8	Winchester Web Design	Staff Party	6/17	300
9	iJams	Training	6/21	450

Format the Worksheet

3. Use **AutoFit** to adjust all four **columns A–D**.

4. Select the **range A3:D3** and apply **Center** alignment.

5. With the headings still selected, apply the Fill Color **Gold, Accent 4**.

6. Select **cell A1** and increase the font size to **18**.

7. Select **cell A2** and increase the font size to **14**.

8. Select the **range A1:D3** and apply **Bold** format.

9. Select the **range D4:D9** and apply **Accounting Number Format**.

Create Formulas

10. In **cell E3** enter `Tax` for the heading.

11. In **column E** calculate the tax for all clients at a rate of 7% on the Fees.

12. In **cell F3** enter `Total` for the heading.

13. In **column F** add the Taxes to the Fees to find the Total for each customer.

14. In **cell G3** enter `Deposit` for the heading.

15. In **column G** calculate the down payment each client paid, which is 20% of the Total after Tax.

16. In **cell H3** enter `Owing` for the heading.

17. In **column H** calculate the amount each client still owes, which is the Total less the Deposit.

18. Select the **range A3:H3** and apply a **Top** and **Bottom** Border.

19. Use the **Scale to Fit** option to ensure the worksheet Width is **one page** when it prints.

20. Save the workbook and close Excel.

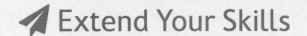

Extend Your Skills

These exercises challenge you to think critically and apply your new skills. You will be evaluated on your ability to follow directions, completeness, creativity, and the use of proper grammar and mechanics. Save files to your chapter folder. Submit assignments as directed.

E1-E1   That's the Way I See It

You would like to take control of your personal finances, and with your newly learned Excel skills you are going to make yourself a monthly budget. Start a new workbook and save it with the name **E1-E1-Budget**. Create a suitable title at the top of your worksheet. Below the title insert **Starting Budget** and then next to that cell enter the amount of money you have to spend each month. Then create three column headings: **Expense**, **Budget Amount**, and **Money Left**. In each row enter the name of the expense and how much you might spend on that item. Then take the Starting Budget and subtract the Budget Amount to find out how much you have left. Repeat this for each row, for as many categories as you need, each time taking the previous amount of Money Left and subtracting the Budget Amount in the current row.

Include at least five expenses, such as Rent, Groceries, and Transportation. Adjust the column widths as necessary and apply appropriate formatting of your choice. Save your workbook.

E1-E2   Be Your Own Boss

As the owner of Blue Jean Landscaping, you need to create an inventory list of equipment you own for your insurance company. Create a new blank workbook and save it with the name **E1-E2-Equipment**. Your insurance company has asked for the following information to be included: Item Name, Value, Number, and a Total for each item.

Set up your worksheet with the company name and the title *Equipment Inventory*, followed by the column headings. Fill in the list with eight to ten items that are standard equipment for a Landscape company. Your list should include items such as rakes, wheelbarrows, and shovels (use an online search if necessary). List their approximate value and how many you own. Then use a formula to find the Total value for each item. Format the Total with dollar signs and apply other formatting as you see fit. Make it look professional, as you will be submitting this to the insurance company, and your Excel worksheet will represent your company. Save your workbook.

E1-E3   Demonstrate Proficiency

Stormy BBQ is known for its delicious, world-famous BBQ sauce. The company would like you to take its secret recipe and create a digital version in Excel. They would also like you to add a multiplier to quickly see how much of each ingredient is needed for larger batches. Begin by saving your file as **E1-E3-Recipe**, inserting an appropriate title, and then adding headings for **Ingredients**, **Cups**, **Batch Multiplier**, and **New Amount**. Use an online search to help you find a recipe for BBQ sauce. List at least six ingredients, such as tomato sauce, brown sugar, vinegar, and mustard. Beside each item insert the amount needed in cups only (estimate the amount needed using your online search; decimals are okay). Then below the Batch Multiplier heading, insert the number **1** and copy it all the way down. Below the *New Amount* heading *customer*, you can now create formulas in each row to multiply the Cups by the Multiplier to get the New Amount needed. Test out your multiplier by increasing the Batch Multiplier and seeing how much of each ingredient you need.

Make any formatting changes you see fit and save your workbook.

EXCEL

2

Recording Student Grades

I n this chapter, you will use Excel to work with multiple worksheets created to record student grades. You will learn about managing and organizing worksheets to insert, delete, or even hide data and also make your data easier to find. You will also learn about using functions in your formulas and the difference between a relative and an absolute reference.

LEARNING OBJECTIVES

▸ Rearrange data on a worksheet

▸ Manage multiple worksheets

▸ Use functions to perform calculations

▸ Use relative and absolute cell references in formulas

▸ Define names for cells and ranges

Project: Tracking Progress

LearnFast College is a school that provides fast-paced learning programs for college students. As an instructor there, you need to keep track of your student grades for an Introduction to Business course. Excel will help you record marks and quickly calculate final grades for the course using a variety of formulas.

Rearrange Data on a Worksheet

When using a worksheet there may be times when you need to do more than simply enter data row by row. You may need to insert more information in the middle of existing data, remove chunks of data already entered, or move cells or entire sections of data around. You can also sort your data to put it into a more usable arrangement.

Insert and Delete Rows, Columns, and Cells

To add more data into your existing data, it might make sense to insert a new cell, column, or row. You can add one cell, row, or column at a time, or several at once. Columns are inserted to the left of your selected column and rows are inserted above your selected row. Inserting a cell or cells allows you to choose to shift the existing data either right or down.

≡ Home→Cells→Insert 🖼 │ Right-click column/row heading→Insert

≡ Home→Cells→Delete 🖼 │ Right-click column/row heading→Delete

DEVELOP YOUR SKILLS: E2-D1

In this exercise, you will insert and delete both rows and columns and insert cells to enter additional student data into the gradebook.

1. Start Excel, open **E2-D1-Grades** from your **Excel Chapter 2** folder, and save it as **E2-D1-NewGrades**.

2. Select the cell with *Pedro's* name, **cell A12**, and choose **Home→Cells→Insert** 🖼 **menu button ▼→Insert Sheet Rows**.

   The data for rows 12:17 is shifted down to rows 13:18, and a blank row is inserted in row 12, the currently selected row.

3. Enter the following data for a new student in **row 12**:

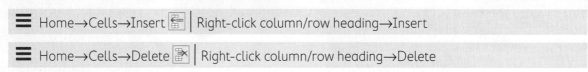

First	Last	Student ID#	Quiz 1	Quiz 2	Quiz Total	Project 1	Project 2
Robert	Moreira	53846	96	88		90	95

Now you will remove a student who is no longer in the class.

4. Select the cell with *Todd's* name, **cell A15**, and then choose **Home→Cells→Delete** menu button ▼→**Delete Sheet Rows**.

All of Todd's information is removed from row 15, and the information from row 16 is shifted up into row 15. Now you need to add a third Quiz score between columns E and F.

5. Follow these steps to insert a new column between **columns E** and **F**:

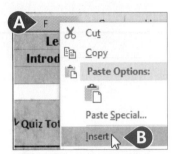

Ⓐ Right-click the **column F** heading.

Ⓑ Choose **Insert** from the menu.

A new column is entered where column F was, and column F is shifted right to become column G.

6. Select the cell with the *Quiz 2* heading, **cell E5**, and use the fill handle to drag one cell to the right, inserting the heading name `Quiz 3` into **cell F5**.

Now you will insert a single cell for a new column heading.

7. Select the cell with *Exam* heading, **cell K5**, and then choose **Home→Cells→Insert** ▦→**Insert Cells**.

8. In the Insert dialog box, choose **Shift Cells Right** and then click **OK**.

The Exam *heading is shifted right into cell L5.*

9. With **cell K5** still selected, type `Participation` as the new heading and then complete the entry.

10. Save the workbook.

Hide and Unhide Rows and Columns

Sometime you may want to save data in your worksheet but have the information in certain rows or columns hidden from view. For example, a retailer might use an item's cost in one column to calculate the sale price in another. The cost column can be hidden from view to prevent customers from seeing how much profit the retailer is making, but the information is still saved and can still be used in a formula. Hidden rows and columns will not print, and a hidden row or column can easily be made visible using Unhide.

Hidden rows and columns can be identified by the gap in the column or row headings, as shown in the figure below.

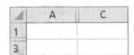

Row 2 and column B are hidden.

☰ Home→Cells→Format ▦→Hide & Unhide | Right-click column/row heading→Hide/Unhide

Sort Data by Column

Excel can easily sort your data in either alphabetic or numeric order, using any column of data. For example, you might want to sort by name, date, item number, or dollar amount. A sort keeps any adjacent data with the row, so data such as the address or phone numbers stays with the name.

≡ Home→Editing→Sort & Filter 🔽

DEVELOP YOUR SKILLS: E2-D2

In this exercise, you will hide and unhide a column and then sort the students by first name.

1. Save your workbook as **E2-D2-NewGrades**.

2. Point to the column heading for **column C**, right-click, and choose **Hide**.

   The Student ID# *column is hidden from view, and now columns B and D are side by side.*

3. Select **cell A6** and then choose **Home→Editing→Sort & Filter 🔽→Sort A to Z 🔽**.

   Ashley is now the first student listed, Sarah is listed last, and all of the corresponding grades for each student are sorted along with the student names.

4. Point to the **column B** heading, press and hold the left mouse button, and then drag to the right to select **columns B:D**.

   Be sure to drag and not to select each column separately because to unhide columns or rows, you must select a continuous *range surrounding the hidden column or row.*

   After columns B:D are selected, there is no line separating the selected range.

5. Choose **Home→Cells→Format 🔳→Hide & Unhide→Unhide Columns**.

   Column C is once again displayed between columns B and D.

6. Save the workbook.

Managing Multiple Worksheets

By default, an Excel workbook contains one worksheet. You can however add multiple worksheets to be saved in the same workbook. This can make it easier to access different worksheets that are related to the same topic. You can also organize a workbook by deleting worksheets you don't need anymore, renaming the worksheets and changing the color of the sheet tab, and moving worksheets.

Insert and Delete Worksheets

Adding a new worksheet is as simple as clicking on the New Sheet button at the bottom of a workbook.

To delete a worksheet, you have to be more careful because, once deleted, you can't recover any of the data from the removed worksheet. Even the Undo button can't fix that problem. For safety, Excel does ask you to confirm the action to delete a worksheet, but only if the worksheet does in fact contain data. A good practice is to save your workbook before deleting a worksheet so there is still a recoverable version if you later change your mind.

≡ Home→Cells→Insert 🖼 menu button ▼→Insert Sheet | Right-click sheet tab→Insert Sheet

≡ Home→Cells→Delete 🖻 menu button ▼→Delete Sheet | Right-click sheet tab→Delete

Rename Worksheets

The default names for your worksheets don't really help someone understand what data is on the worksheet or what it is being used for. When you start adding more and more worksheets, you need to quickly find the sheet with the information you need, so it becomes important to name your sheets.

Names should be short and describe the purpose of the worksheet as clearly as possible. Certain characters, such as ? and /, are restricted, so it is best to stick to text and numbers. To rename a sheet, simply double-click the sheet tab and type the new name.

| Cash Flow | Revenue | Expenses | **Summary** | ⊕ |

Examples of good worksheet names that are short, simple, and descriptive

≡ Home→Cells→Format→Rename Sheet | Double-click Sheet tab

DEVELOP YOUR SKILLS: E2-D3

In this exercise, you will insert a new sheet, delete a sheet, and rename a sheet.

1. Save your workbook as **E2-D3-NewGrades**.

2. Follow these steps to insert a new worksheet:

Ⓐ Click the **New Sheet** button.

Ⓑ Notice that a new worksheet is inserted to the right of the active sheet, **New**. The default worksheet name is **Sheet** with a number, which continues to increase each time you add a new sheet.

Ⓒ Click on the **old** worksheet tab to activate the sheet.

3. Choose **Home→Cells→Delete** 🖻 **menu button** ▼→**Delete Sheet** and click the **Delete** button or tap ⏎Enter when prompted in the dialog box.

   Because there was text on the old worksheet, Excel asks you to confirm before it will delete and permanently remove the sheet.

4. Double-click the **Sheet1** tab that was just created, type **Participation**, and then tap ⏎Enter.

5. Change the name of the **New** worksheet to **Final Grades**.

6. Select the title in the merged **cell A2** and press ⌈Ctrl⌉+⌈C⌉ to copy the title *Introduction to Business*.

7. Click the **Participation** worksheet tab, ensure **cell A1** is the selected cell, and press ⌈Ctrl⌉+⌈V⌉ to paste the text.

8. Select **cell A2** below the class title, type **Participation Grades**, and then tap ⌈Enter⌉.

9. Select **cell A1**, choose **Home→Clipboard→Format Painter** ✎, and then click **cell A2** to apply the formatting from cell A1.

    Clicking Format Painter once allows you to apply the formatting once, and then it is turned off. If you wanted to continue applying the same formatting to more cells or ranges, you would double-click the Format Painter instead.

    The range A2:M2 is merged and centered, and the text now has the same formatting as the title.

10. Save the workbook.

Move a Worksheet

To organize your sheets better, you may want to rearrange the order of the sheets at the bottom of the workbook. Excel doesn't have a feature for sorting worksheets, but you can simply drag worksheet tabs left or right to rearrange the order. You can also rearrange or duplicate the sheets using the Move or Copy dialog box.

≡ Home→Cells→Format→Move or Copy Sheet │ Right click worksheet tab→Move or Copy Sheet

Change the Worksheet Tab Color

Finding the right worksheet can also be a lot quicker if you use a system of colors for different worksheets. Colors could be assigned based on department, function, importance, or any method you choose. Adding a color to a worksheet tab is available from the Ribbon or by right-clicking the tab.

These are some examples of using Tab Colors to organize worksheets; notice the selected worksheet appears only lightly shaded.

≡ Home→Cells→Format→Tab Color │ Right-click worksheet tab→Tab Color

Hide a Worksheet

Similar to hiding rows and columns, you may want to save a worksheet's information but have it hidden from view. Hiding a worksheet can also help organize your workbook if you have a lot of tabs or if the end-user will use only some of the worksheets. In this case, hiding the unused worksheets makes it a more user-friendly workbook. Once hidden, it is easy enough to unhide a worksheet when you need to use it again.

≡ Home→Cells→Format→Hide & Unhide │ Right-click worksheet tab→Hide/Unhide

In this exercise, you will reorganize and color the worksheet tabs.

1. Save your workbook as **E2-D4-NewGrades**.

2. Follow these steps to move the Final Grades worksheet and add a tab color:

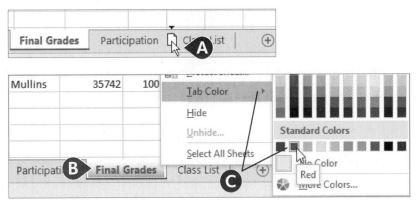

🄐 Drag the **Final Grades** sheet to the right side past the **Participation** sheet as shown here.

Notice the small black arrow follows your cursor indicating the new position for the sheet you are moving.

🄑 Right-click the **Final Grades** sheet.

🄒 Choose **Tab Color→Standard Color Red**.

3. Change the color of the **Participation** sheet tab to **Standard Color Blue**.

The Class List worksheet is not needed at this time, so you will hide it.

4. Right-click the **Class List** worksheet tab and choose **Hide**.

5. Save the workbook.

Create a Cell Reference to Another Worksheet

When using multiple worksheets, you can use common information across different sheets. Excel allows you to link cells from different worksheets in the same workbook or in other workbooks. Linking places values from a source worksheet into a destination worksheet. For example, you may want to have a revenue worksheet and a profit worksheet; the profit worksheet can use the values from the revenue worksheet. If the revenue worksheet values ever change, the profit worksheet values will update automatically.

Referencing another worksheet requires the actual cell reference as well as the worksheet name and an exclamation point as shown below. Cell references to other workbooks require the workbook name, sheet name, and cell reference. Cell references to other worksheets or workbooks can be used to simply link the data or can be used in a formula.

A3 is the cell reference on the Revenue worksheet.

In this example, the Revenue worksheet is in a different workbook, and the name of the workbook, *2015Financial.xlsx*, is placed inside square brackets.

=Revenue!A3

=[2015Financial.xlsx]Revenue!A3

Revenue is the name of the worksheet in the current workbook, followed by an exclamation point.

EXCEL

It is possible to manually type a cell reference to another worksheet or workbook; however, it is simpler and much more accurate to use the point-and-click method. If you point and click, Excel inserts all of the necessary formatting, such as brackets and exclamation points.

DEVELOP YOUR SKILLS: E2-D5

In this exercise, you will use linking formulas to add student names to a worksheet.

1. Save your workbook as **E2-D5-NewGrades**.
2. Activate the **Participation** worksheet by clicking its tab and then select **cell A4**.
3. Enter the heading **First** in **cell A4**, tap Tab, enter the heading **Last** in **cell B4**, and tap Enter.
4. In **cell A5** type = and then click the **Final Grades** worksheet tab.

   Notice that you are looking at the Final Grades worksheet now; however, the Formula Bar shows the beginning of the formula you are entering on the Participation worksheet, including the Final Grades worksheet name.

   Excel adds single quotes around any worksheet name that contains a space.

5. Select **cell A6** and then click **Enter** ✓ on the Formula Bar.

   Completing the entry this way and NOT clicking the Participation worksheet tab is very important, because doing so would change your formula. Completing the entry instantly brings you back to the Participation worksheet. You will now see the name Ashley in cell A5 and the formula ='Final Grades'!A6 in the Formula Bar.

6. With **cell A5** still selected, use the fill handle to drag one cell to the right, inserting the last name for Ashley into **cell B5**.
7. With the **range A5:B5** selected (the cells with Ashley's first and last names), drag the fill handle down to **row 16**.

   The names for all twelve students are now added to the Participation worksheet, and if the names are edited on the Final Grades worksheet, changes will automatically be updated on the Participation worksheet. Felecia has informed the school the correct spelling of her name is "Felicia," so you will update this now.

8. Go to the **Final Grades** sheet and select *Felecia's* first name in **cell A10**.
9. Edit the name by changing the second *e* to an **i** and then complete the entry.
10. Go back to the **Participation** worksheet and notice Felicia's name has now been updated in **cell A9**.

11. Save the workbook.

Create a Copy of a Worksheet

Rather than starting with a new blank worksheet, you can save a lot of time by using an existing worksheet that already has some of the information you need or has the structure and formatting you want. Creating a copy of a worksheet does not affect the original worksheet. The new worksheet will have the same name but with *(2)* added to the end to indicate it is a second version.

≡ Home→Cells→Format→Move or Copy Sheet │ Right-click worksheet tab→Move or Copy Sheet

Edit Multiple Sheets at One Time

It is also possible to select several worksheets at the same time. While multiple sheets are selected you can modify all of the selected sheets by making changes to one of them. You can enter text or formulas or change cell format in the same cell in all of the selected sheets simultaneously. You need to be very careful with this feature, however, to ensure you are not replacing existing data in one of the worksheets you can't see!

Multiple sheets can be selected (or grouped) by holding the Ctrl key while clicking additional sheet tabs. To deselect (or ungroup) the multiple worksheets, either select a different sheet or right-click one of the sheet tabs and choose Ungroup Sheets.

DEVELOP YOUR SKILLS: E2-D6

In this exercise, you will create a new worksheet by copying the Participation sheet and make changes to both at once.

1. Save your workbook as **E2-D6-NewGrades**.
2. Right-click the **Participation** worksheet tab and choose **Move or Copy**.
3. Click the checkbox to select **Create a Copy.** Under Before Sheet choose **Move to End** and **OK**.

   The new worksheet is created to the right of the Final Grades sheet; it is identical to Participation and named Participation (2).
4. Right-click the **Participation** sheet tab again and choose **Move or Copy**.
5. This time *do not* click the Create a Copy box. Under Before Sheet choose **Participation (2)** and **OK**.

   The original Participation sheet is now positioned to the right of the Final Grades sheet, before the Participation (2) sheet.
6. Double-click the **Participation (2)** sheet tab, rename it **Exam**, and then tap Enter .

   Your sheet tabs should now look like this.

7. Select the merged **cell A2** and double-click the word *Participation* in the Formula Bar.

   This method of editing cell contents allows you to replace part of the cell without retyping the whole thing.
8. Type **Exam** and complete the entry, so the subtitle in **cell A2** now reads *Exam Grades*.

Edit Multiple Sheets at Once

Now you will select both the Participation and Exam worksheets to edit them both at once because you want the same changes applied to both.

9. With the *Exam* worksheet still active, press and hold the ⎡Ctrl⎤ key and click the **Participation** worksheet tab.

   Both worksheets are now selected, their names are both bold, and there is a thick line below both sheet tabs. The Final Grades worksheet is not selected.

10. With both sheets selected and the *Exam* worksheet still active, select the **range A4:B4**.

11. Apply **Bold** format, increase the Font Size to **12**, and apply **Center** alignment.

12. Add a **Thick Bottom Border** and Fill Color **Green, Accent 6, Lighter 40%** (last column, fourth row).

13. Click the **Participation** worksheet tab to confirm your changes were made to both sheets and then click the **Final Grades** worksheet tab to deselect the other two sheets.

14. Save the workbook.

Using Functions in Formulas

Functions are an important part of Excel. Functions allow you to do much more than simple mathematical operations. For example, adding two or three cells would not be a problem; however, if you needed to add hundreds or even thousands of cells, it would be quite the tedious task to use a formula such as =A1+A2+A3+A4... and so on. The Sum Function allows you to specify a range instead of individual cells, and then the function tells Excel what operation to perform on the range, in this case addition.

Functions can be typed directly into the cell or inserted in a number of ways. Functions are available from the Formulas tab, by using AutoSum, or by using Insert Function. The most common functions are available in the AutoSum drop-down menu. Formulas with functions are typically made up of the function name and one or more arguments. An argument is the name for the numbers, cells, or ranges that are used in the function.

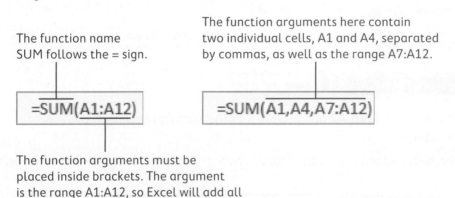

The function name
SUM follows the = sign.

The function arguments here contain
two individual cells, A1 and A4, separated
by commas, as well as the range A7:A12.

=SUM(A1:A12)

=SUM(A1,A4,A7:A12)

The function arguments must be
placed inside brackets. The argument
is the range A1:A12, so Excel will add all
of the values contained in that range.

Use the AutoSum Feature

The AutoSum feature not only makes it easy to find some of the simplest functions, but it also helps identify and enter the range of cells you are most likely to use in your function. Often when you have a column of numbers, you want to add a total at the bottom of the column. In a row, the total would be placed on the right side of the row.

AutoSum will automatically search for adjacent data, either directly above or to the left of the selected cell. Therefore, selecting the cell at the bottom of a column or the right side of a row and clicking AutoSum will very quickly enter the SUM function, which will add all of the numbers in that column or row. If necessary, you can alter the range that Excel has selected by dragging to select the desired cells before completing the entry. Another option is to select the data in the row or column first and then click AutoSum.

Sum, Average, Count, Max, and Min

The Sum function is just one of the AutoSum options; other frequently used functions can also be found via the AutoSum drop-down menu. These functions will take a set of numbers identified in the arguments and find the average, locate the highest or lowest value, or simply count how many numbers are in the set. Similar to AutoSum, these functions will automatically search for adjacent data, either directly above or to the left of the selected cell.

AUTOSUM FUNCTIONS

Function Name	Description
SUM	Adds the values in the cells
AVERAGE	Calculates the average of the values in the cells
COUNT	Counts the number of cells that contain numerical values; cells containing text and blank cells are ignored
MAX	Returns the highest value
MIN	Returns the lowest value

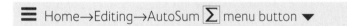 Home→Editing→AutoSum Σ menu button ▼

Use Insert Function

For more complex functions, the Insert Function button opens up a dialog box that allows you to explore options and enter arguments. In the Insert Function dialog box, you can search by keyword or browse by category. After choosing the function, the Function Arguments dialog box opens, which allows you to enter the numbers, cell references, or criteria to use in the function.

 View the video "Entering a Formula Using the Insert Function."

In this exercise, you will insert functions to calculate the total each student earned on projects and quizzes and the average grade in the class.

1. Save your workbook as **E2-D7-NewGrades**.
2. On the **Final Grades** worksheet, select the empty cell under *Project Total* for the first student, **cell J6**.

   This is the cell where you will calculate a sum.
3. Choose **Home→Editing→AutoSum** Σ.

   The Sum function is entered into cell J6. Excel finds two adjacent cells to the left of cell J6 containing numerical data, so the range H6:I6 is automatically entered into the brackets.

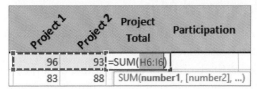

4. Click **Enter** ✓ to finish the entry, and the result of the formula displayed in **cell J6** is *189*.
5. Use the fill handle to copy the formula in **cell J6** down the column for the rest of the students.

   The students have not done Quiz 3 yet, but you can enter the formula to add the grades from the three quizzes now. Then when grades for Quiz 3 are entered, it will automatically calculate the sum of all three.
6. Follow these steps to enter the SUM function for the three quizzes:

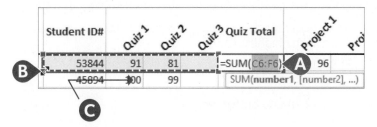

   Ⓐ Select **cell G6** under the heading Quiz Total and choose **Home→Editing→AutoSum** Σ.

   This time the AutoSum feature finds four cells adjacent to the left of cell G6 and includes all four. This is incorrect because column C contains the Student ID#, not a Quiz to include in our Sum, so you will adjust the range.

   Ⓑ Move the mouse pointer over the sizing handle in the bottom-left corner of **cell C6** to display the resize pointer.

   Ⓒ Drag the handle right to the bottom left of **cell D6**, ensure the formula displays *=SUM(D6:F6)*, and click Enter on the Formula Bar.

   The formula now displays in the Formula Bar and the result 172 displays in cell G6.
7. Use the fill handle in **cell G6** to copy the formula down the column for the rest of the students.

   Notice that a warning displays in the top-left corner of the cells that contain the formula, indicating your formula omits adjacent cells. Because this is the correct formula, the warning can be ignored and removed.

8. Follow these steps to remove the error:

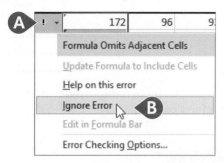

Ⓐ Point to the yellow warning sign with the exclamation point and click the **menu** button ▼ that appears.

Ⓑ Choose **Ignore Error** from the list.

Next you want to find the average grade that students received on Quiz 1 and 2, so you will use the AVERAGE function.

9. Select the **range B18:C18** below the last student and choose **Home→Alignment→Merge & Center**.

10. In the merged cell enter the text `Class Average` and tap Tab .

11. In **cell D18** choose **Home→Editing→AutoSum Σ menu button ▼→Average**.

The AVERAGE function is inserted, and because the adjacent cells above the active cell contain numerical values, Excel chooses the range D6:D17 automatically.

12. Complete the entry in **cell D18** and then use the fill handle to copy the average formula from **cell D18** to the right into **cell E18**.

13. Select the **range B18:E18** (the averages and the row heading) and apply **Bold** format.

14. The class average functions should now look like this.

Class Average	88.917	87.583

15. Save the workbook and close Excel.

Understanding Relative and Absolute Cell References

Cell references make it easier to copy formulas when you want to reuse the same formula structure. A relative cell reference is one in which the location of the cell remains relative to the cell that contains the formula. For example, if the formula =A3-B3 is in cell C3, the relative position of A3 is two cells to the left of C3, and B3 is one cell to the left of C3.

When you copy the formula to another cell, the cell references will change to be in the same position relatively. So if you copy the formula down to the next row in cell C4, the new formula is =A4-B4. Excel updates the new cell references so they are in the same relative position in regards to cell C4; that is, two cells to the left and one cell to the left.

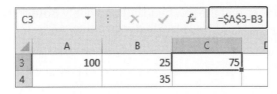

The original formula is seen in the Formula Bar, with relative references to both cells A3 and B3.

The copied formula is displayed with the new cell references A4 and B4.

 View the Video "Using Relative and Absolute Cell References."

Absolute Cell References

In some situations, you do *not* want the cell reference to change when you move or copy the formula. To ensure the cell reference does not change, you can use an absolute cell reference. You can think of an absolute cell reference as being "locked in place"; that is, the cell reference will not change when copied. To make a cell reference absolute, you take a relative cell reference such as A1 and add a dollar sign in front of the column and row component of the cell reference so it looks like this: $A$1. If the formula =$A$3-B3 is entered in cell C3 and then copied to cell C4, the formula in cell C4 would then be =$A$3-B4. $A$3 is an absolute reference, so it does not change, and B3 is a relative reference, so it changes to B4.

To create an absolute cell reference, you simply type the cell reference and include the dollar signs in front of the column and row references. Alternatively, you can click to select the cell you want to use in the reference and then tap the F4 key on the keyboard, which will insert both dollar signs into the cell reference.

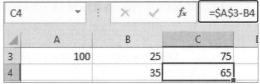

The original formula is seen in the Formula Bar and contains an absolute reference to cell $A$3.

After the formula is copied, the absolute reference $A$3 does not change.

Mixed Cell References

You can also mix relative and absolute references. For example, $A3 is a reference to cell A3 where the column reference is absolute (the column will not change when copied) and the row reference is relative (it will change when copied). This can be useful when copying a formula both across a row and down a column.

After you have tapped the F4 key once, tapping it a second time will make the absolute reference a mixed reference with only a $ sign in front of the row reference. A third tap of F4 places the $ in front of only the column reference, and a fourth tap removes all $ signs so it is again a relative reference.

Display and Print Formulas

To see a formula you have entered, you must select the cell first, and then the Formula Bar displays the formula while the result of the formula is displayed in the worksheet. This means that to check your formulas, you would have to click each cell and check them one at a time. However, when you have many cells with formulas, this would be very hard to do. An easier way is to display all formulas at once. When you choose to display formulas, Excel automatically widens columns to show more of the cell contents. You can also edit the formulas or print the worksheet while the formulas are displayed.

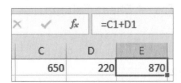

Normally the cell must be selected for you to see the formula.

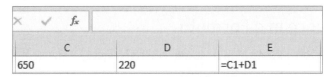

After clicking Show Formulas, the formula displays in the worksheet without you selecting the cell.

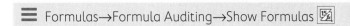

Formulas→Formula Auditing→Show Formulas 🔢

DEVELOP YOUR SKILLS: E2-D8

In this exercise, you will use formulas with absolute references to find the percentage grade each student scored on the exam.

1. Open **E2-D8-NewGrades** from your **Excel Chapter 2** folder and save it as **E2-D8-NewGradesRevised**.

2. Ensure you are on the **Exam** worksheet and insert a formula in **cell H5** that will add up the five different sections of the exam. (Hint: Use AutoSum.)

3. Copy the formula in **cell H5** down the column for the rest of the students.

   The totals calculated here will be used to calculate the final grades, so now you will create a reference to these totals on the Final Grades worksheet.

4. Go to the **Final Grades** worksheet and select **cell L6**.

5. Type **=** and click the **Exam** worksheet tab, select **cell H5**, and complete the entry.

6. Copy the formula in **cell L6** down the column for the other students.

   The totals on the Exam worksheet should be identical to the totals on the Final Grades worksheet, as shown for the first few students below.

Total /150
123
120
125

Total column
on the Exam
worksheet.

Exam
123
120
125

Exam grades on
the Final Grades
sheet

7. Select **cell L6** and choose **Home→Cells→Insert→Insert Sheet Rows**.

8. Select the **range A6:M6** and apply the **Thick Bottom Border**.

9. In **cell C6** enter `Out Of` for the row heading.

10. In **cell G6** enter 300, in **cell J6** enter 200, and in **cell L6** enter 150.

11. Select **cell M5** and choose **Home→Cells→Insert→Insert Sheet Column**.

12. In **cell M5** enter `Exam %` for the column heading.

Your headings should now look like this.

Student ID#	Quiz 1	Quiz 2	Quiz 3	Quiz Total	Project 1	Project 2	Project Total	Participation	Exam	Exam %	Final Grade
Out Of				300			200		150		

Use an Absolute Reference in a Formula

13. Follow these steps to enter a formula with an absolute cell reference:

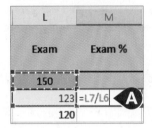 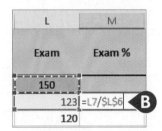

Ⓐ In **cell M7** enter the formula **=L7/L6** but *do not* complete the entry yet.

In this formula, cell L7 is the exam grade for Ashley, which will change for each student when we copy the formula. Cell L6 is the number of total points the exam is worth, in this case 150, which will not change for each student—therefore cell L6 needs to be an absolute reference. While editing the formula, the insertion point must be immediately before or after the reference to cell L6. Be sure the insertion point is placed correctly or the correct cell reference won't be converted.

Ⓑ While still editing the formula, tap the F4 key on the keyboard, which will make the reference for **cell L6** *absolute* (the $ signs in front of the column and row), and then complete the entry.

The result of the formula is 0.82 for Ashley. (You may see 1 if your results are being rounded.)

14. Apply the **Percent Style** % number format to **cell M7** and copy the formula down the column for the other students.

15. Select **cell M8** to ensure the formula copied correctly; the formula should be *=L8/$L$6* with the result being *80%* for Atif.

Now you will repeat these steps twice, once to calculate the Percent Grade for the Quizzes and once for the Projects.

16. Select **cell H5**, insert a new column, and then enter `Quiz %` as the column heading.

17. Select **cell L5**, insert a column, and enter `Project %` as the column heading.

18. Enter two formulas: In **cell H7** the formula to calculate Quiz percentage is =G7/$G$6, and in **cell L7** the formula for Project percentage is =K7/$K$6.

19. Use the **Format Painter** to copy the format from the Exam % column to the two formulas you just entered and then copy the formula down both columns.

Your worksheet should now look like the image below.

First	Last	Student ID#	Quiz 1	Quiz 2	Quiz 3	Quiz Total	Quiz %	Project 1	Project 2	Project Total	Project %	Participation	Exam	Exam %	Final Grade
						LearnFast College									
						Introduction to Business									
						Sep-16									
		Out Of				300				200			150		
Ashley	Ronayne	53844	91	81		172	57%	96	93	189	95%		123	82%	
Atif	Khalil	45894	100	99		199	66%	83	88	171	86%		120	80%	
Austin	Farrell	50572	81	85		166	55%	94	89	183	92%		125	83%	
Crystal	Robinson	47088	92	81		173	58%	80	95	175	88%		132	88%	
Felicia	Murray	45003	88	87		175	58%	87	82	169	85%		130	87%	
Jessica	McInnis	45537	85	93		178	59%	81	99	180	90%		116	77%	
John	Aikens	51028	93	82		175	58%	94	100	194	97%		116	77%	
Linda	Jefferies	39695	80	95		175	58%	91	88	179	90%		133	89%	
Pamela	Clark	46389	65	83		148	49%	62	90	152	76%		132	88%	
Pedro	Espinosa	37059	96	94		190	63%	86	96	182	91%		130	87%	
Robert	Moreira	53846	96	88		184	61%	90	95	185	93%		130	87%	
Sarah	Mullins	35742	100	83		183	61%	85	89	174	87%		120	80%	
	Class Average		88.917	87.583											

20. Save the workbook.

Define Names for Cells and Ranges

When you refer to the same cell or range of cells repeatedly in your formulas, it can be more efficient if you create a name for the cell or range. It is easier to remember a name than to scroll or click around your workbook looking for the cells you want to use. This is especially true if you are using a cell or range from another worksheet or workbook.

Cell names *cannot* contain spaces. Names can be created directly in the Name Box or from the Formulas tab on the ribbon. You can also create, edit, or delete cell names using the Name Manager.

Note! *Name references are also absolute cell references; that is to say, the reference will not change when moved or copied.*

The cell name in the Name Box,
TaxRate (does not contain a space),
refers to cell B2.

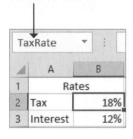

≡ Formulas→Defined Names

Use a Cell Name in a Formula

When using a cell name in a formula, it works just like any other cell reference. The cell name can be typed, or the cell can be selected with the mouse. You can also begin to type the first few letters of the name and then double-click the name from the AutoComplete list that appears.

Typing the beginning of the cell name will bring up suggested names.

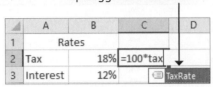

The formula, after the cell name has been inserted, highlights the cell named *TaxRate*.

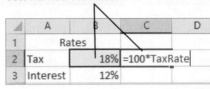

The formula's result is displayed; 100 multiplied by 18% is *18*.

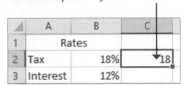

DEVELOP YOUR SKILLS: E2-D9

In this exercise, you will create names for cells and then enter formulas using those names for the cell references.

1. Save your workbook as **E2-D9-NewGrades**.
2. Enter the following data in the **range A21:B25**:

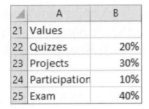

3. Select **cell B22** and choose **Formulas→Defined Names→Define Name** ⊟.

   Notice that Excel adds text into the Name section for you based on the adjacent cell.

4. Ensure that **Quizzes** is inserted in the Name section at the top of the dialog box and then click **OK**.
5. Select **cell B23** and name the cell **Projects**.
6. For **cell B24** and **cell B25**, name the cells **Participation** and **Exam**, respectively.
7. Choose **Formulas→Defined Names→Name Manager** 🖼 to open the dialog box and make sure that all four names have been added as shown here:

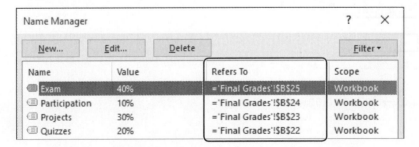

Note the Refers To section indicates the Final Grades worksheet and the cells B22, B23, B24, and B25, with absolute references

8. Select **cell P5**, insert a new column, and then add the heading **Weighted Exam Mark** to the new column in **cell P5**.

9. Use **Wrap Text** to fit the *Weighted Exam Mark* heading into **cell P5** on two lines.

Use Cell Names in Formulas

10. Select **cell P6**, enter the formula **=Exam**, and then click **Enter** ✓.

    The formula takes the value from the cell named Exam, 0.4 or 40%, and enters the value in cell P6.

11. Apply the **%** Number Format to **cell P6** and then tap Enter.

12. In **cell P7** enter the formula **=O7*Exam** (O7 is the cell reference, O as in octopus) and then click **Enter** ✓.

    The mark for the first student, Ashley, is 33% out of 40% for the Exam part of her grade.

13. Fill the formula in **cell P7** down the column for the remaining students.

14. Your worksheet should now look like the following.

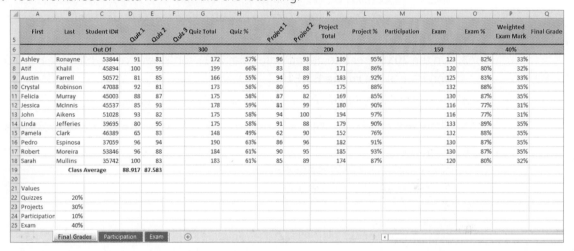

	First	Last	Student ID#	Quiz 1	Quiz 2	Quiz 3	Quiz Total	Quiz %	Project 1	Project 2	Project Total	Project %	Participation	Exam	Exam %	Weighted Exam Mark	Final Grade
6			Out Of				300				200			150		40%	
7	Ashley	Ronayne	53844	91	81		172	57%	96	93	189	95%		123	82%	33%	
8	Atif	Khalil	45894	100	99		199	66%	83	88	171	86%		120	80%	32%	
9	Austin	Farrell	50572	81	85		166	55%	94	89	183	92%		125	83%	33%	
10	Crystal	Robinson	47088	92	81		173	58%	80	95	175	88%		132	88%	35%	
11	Felicia	Murray	45003	88	87		175	58%	87	82	169	85%		130	87%	35%	
12	Jessica	McInnis	45537	85	93		178	59%	81	99	180	90%		116	77%	31%	
13	John	Aikens	51028	93	82		175	58%	94	100	194	97%		116	77%	31%	
14	Linda	Jefferies	39695	80	95		175	58%	91	88	179	90%		133	89%	35%	
15	Pamela	Clark	46389	65	83		148	49%	62	90	152	76%		132	88%	35%	
16	Pedro	Espinosa	37059	96	94		190	63%	86	96	182	91%		130	87%	35%	
17	Robert	Moreira	53846	96	88		184	61%	90	95	185	93%		130	87%	35%	
18	Sarah	Mullins	35742	100	83		183	61%	85	89	174	87%		120	80%	32%	
19		Class Average		88.917	87.583												
20																	
21	Values																
22	Quizzes	20%															
23	Projects	30%															
24	Participation	10%															
25	Exam	40%															

Final Grades | Participation | Exam

15. Save the workbook and close Excel.

Self-Assessment

Check your knowledge of this chapter's key concepts and skills using the Self-Assessment in your ebook or eLab course.

Reinforce Your Skills

Use Formulas to Find Total and Average

In this exercise, you will create a copy of a worksheet that Kids for Change used to calculate expense reimbursements paid out to volunteers in 2015 and update the sheet for 2016.

1. Start Excel, open **E2-R1-Volunteers** from your **Excel Chapter 2** folder, and save it as **E2-R1-Volunteers2016**.

   Because many of the volunteers are the same each year, and you want to use the same basic structure for the worksheet, it is easier to create a copy then to start all over.

2. Create a copy of the **2015** sheet and rename it **2016**.

   The 2015 sheet did not use formulas for the calculations, so the data can be deleted. However, after your sheet contains the proper formulas, you delete the input data only, leaving formulas such as Total for the next year's calculations.

3. On the **2016** sheet delete all data from 2015 for Miles Driven, Mileage Paid, Other Expenses, and Total in the **range B5:E10**.

4. Cheryl did not volunteer this year, so delete **row 7** from the worksheet.

5. There was a new volunteer in 2016, so enter her name, `Jessica Banderas`, in **cell A10**.

6. Enter the following data under mileage driven for the corresponding volunteers:

4	Name	Miles Driven
5	Dave Lozano	80
6	Sharon Foster	173
7	Brad Bird	96
8	Michelle Smith	164
9	Stewart Schott	205
10	Jessica Banderas	104

7. Sort the volunteers by Miles Driven, from lowest to highest.

   This year you want to calculate and compare the total and average miles driven for all volunteers to last year's total and average mileage, so you will add row headings and formulas to both sheets at once.

8. With the **2016** sheet active, notice **row 11** is the first empty row and then go to the **2015** sheet and ensure **row 11** is also empty.

9. With the **2015** sheet active, select the **2016** sheet as well to edit both at once (remember to use the Ctrl key).

10. Now below the last volunteer, enter `Total` for the heading in **cell A11**.

11. In **cell A12** enter `Average` for the heading.

12. Use Format Painter to copy the formatting from the title in **cell A1** to the headings you just inserted in the **range A11:A12** and then decrease the font size to **12**.

13. With the **2015** and **2016** sheets both still active, use AutoSum to add the total for miles driven in **cell B11**.

14. Insert a formula using the Average function into **cell B12**, being careful to ensure the proper **range B5:B10** is selected (*do not* include the Total in the average calculation).

15. Apply **Bold** format to the **range B11:B12** with the formulas you just created.

16. Go to the **2016** worksheet to see your formulas and notice that the 2015 sheet is no longer active.

17. Change the tab color for the **2016** sheet to **Green, Accent 6** and change the tab color for **2015** to **Blue, Accent 5**.

18. Save the workbook.

REINFORCE YOUR SKILLS: E2-R2

Use Formulas with Absolute References

In this exercise, you will use formulas with absolute references to calculate Mileage Paid to the Kids for Change volunteers and then calculate totals and tax deductions.

1. Save your workbook as **E2-R2-Volunteers2016**.

2. On the **2016** worksheet, select **cell C5** and insert two new sheet rows.

3. In the newly inserted rows, insert the text **Rate:** in **cell C5** and the number **0.25** in **cell C6**.

4. In **cell C7** insert a formula that calculates the miles driven for Dave Lozano times the rate, making sure you use an absolute cell reference to **cell C6** for the rate.

   Cell C6 is an absolute reference because the rate will stay the same for all volunteers when you copy the formula down the column.

5. With **cell C7** selected, copy the formula down the column for the other volunteers.

6. Hide **rows 5** and **6**.

7. Hide the **2015** worksheet.

8. Enter the following amounts under Other Expenses for the volunteers:

4	Name	Miles Driven	Mileage Paid	Other Expenses
7	Dave Lozano	80	20.00	0.00
8	Brad Bird	96	24.00	22.75
9	Jessica Banderas	104	26.00	0.00
10	Michelle Smith	164	41.00	0.00
11	Sharon Foster	173	43.25	32.00
12	Stewart Schott	205	51.25	10.13

9. Create a formula in **cell E7** to calculate the Total, adding the Mileage Paid and Other Expenses.

10. Copy the formula down the column for the other volunteers.

11. Apply **Bold** and the **Currency** number format to the Total amounts in **column E**.

12. Insert a formula using the **Sum** function in **cell E13** that will find a grand total paid out to all volunteers.

13. Below the grand total, in **cell E14**, insert a formula to find the average amount paid to the volunteers.

14. Apply **Bold** to the **range E13:E14** and then add a **Bottom Border** to the range **B12:E12**.

15. In **cell A17** enter the heading **Tax Deduction** and then in **cell A18** enter 70%.

16. Select **cell A18** and name the cell **Tax**.

17. Insert the heading **Tax Deduction** in **cell F4** and then widen the column to **12**.

18. In **cell F7** enter the formula **=E7*Tax** and then copy the formula down the column.

19. Save the workbook and close Excel.

REINFORCE YOUR SKILLS: E2-R3

Format Worksheets and Create Formulas with Functions

In this exercise, you will calculate the Kids for Change employee contributions to an employee retirement savings fund, setting up the appropriate functions, and copy the worksheet to use again the following year.

1. Start Excel, open **E2-R3-Savings** from your **Excel Chapter 2** folder, and save it as **E2-R3-Savings2016**.

2. Begin on the **2015** sheet by calculating the total annual contributions for each employee, using the **Sum** function in **column F**.

3. Apply **Bold** and **Currency** number format and decrease the number of decimals twice to remove the decimal.

4. Insert a new row above *Shannon* to enter a new employee and then enter the name **Ruth Bowers** in the new blank row in **cell A9**.

5. For Ruth's contributions enter the number **0** under Q1, Q2, and Q3 and enter **150** under Q4.
   Notice Excel enters the formula under Annual Total for you.

6. Enter the row heading **Average Per Q** in **cell A12** and then enter a formula in **cell B12** to find the average Quarter 1 (Q1) contributions for all employees.

7. Copy the formula across for Q2, Q3, and Q4 and then apply **Bold** format and reduce the decimals to two decimal places.

8. Use **Format Painter** to copy the format from **cell A4** and apply it to **cell A12**.

9. With the 2015 sheet active, select the **2014** sheet as well to edit both at once and then in **cell D13** enter the heading **2015 Grand Total**.

10. In **cell F13** enter a formula to find the grand total of all employees' annual contributions.

11. Use **Format Painter** to apply the format from **cell A12** to the **range D13:F13** and then apply **Currency** number format and remove both of the decimals in **cell F13**.

12. Go to the **2014** sheet, ensure the sheets are no longer grouped, and edit the heading in **cell D13** to be **2014 Grand Total**.

13. Go back to the **2015** sheet and in **cell D14** enter the heading **Increase from 2014**.

14. In **cell F14** enter a formula to take the grand total from 2015 and divide by the grand total from 2014.

15. Apply the **%** number format to **cell F14**.

16. Hide the **2014** worksheet.

17. In **cell D15** enter **Largest Contribution** and then in **cell D16** enter **Smallest Contribution**.

18. In **cell F15** enter a formula and use the **MAX** function to find the biggest contribution in the **range F5:F11**.

19. In **cell F16** enter a formula and use the **MIN** function to find the smallest number in the same range.

   The company has decided at the end of 2015 to match employee contributions this year by adding 30%, so you will now add this calculation to the worksheet.

20. In **cell G4** enter the heading `Company Amt` and widen the column to fit the heading.

21. Insert a new row above the first employee, *Craig*.

22. In **cell G5** enter **30%** for the company contribution matching rate.

23. In **cell G6** enter a formula to multiply the Annual Total for Craig by the rate in **cell G5** and be sure to use an absolute cell reference for **cell G5**.

24. Copy the formula down the column for the other employees.

25. Hide **row 5**, which contains only the 30% figure.

26. Create a copy of the **2015** worksheet and then rename the new worksheet **2016**.

27. If necessary, move the **2016** worksheet to the right of the **2015** worksheet.

28. On the **2016** sheet, delete all the data from the **range B6:E12** but leave all formulas as they are.

   The 2016 sheet is now ready to use once the data becomes available.

29. Save the workbook and close Excel.

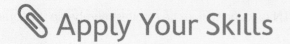 Apply Your Skills

Edit and Format Multiple Sheets

In this exercise, you will take an existing set of prices for Universal Corporate Events services and rearrange some of the data.

1. Start Excel, open **E2-A1-Prices** from your **Excel Chapter 2** folder, and save it as **E2-A1-PricesNew**.

   There is a hidden sheet that does not use formulas or have the correct formatting, so it needs to be removed and recreated.

2. Unhide the existing worksheet called **VIP Price List** and then delete the **VIP Price List** sheet.

3. On the **Price List** sheet, replace the heading **Amount** with the heading **Price**.

4. Create a copy of the **Price List** sheet and rename it **Old Price List**.

5. Hide the **Old Price List** sheet.

6. On the **Price List** sheet, insert a row above **row 3**.

7. Sort the **Services Price List** by Price, from largest to smallest.

8. Insert a column to the left of the *Deposit* column.

9. In **row 4** enter the heading **Price** in the new column and then change the heading in **column B** to **Old Price**.

10. Create a copy of the **Price List** worksheet and rename it **VIP Price List**.

11. Select both worksheets and insert a row above **row 5**.

12. With both worksheets still selected, enter **Price Increase** in **cell A5**.

13. Then in **cell B5** enter **10%**.

14. Apply a **Bottom Border** to the **range A5:D5**.

15. Now select only the **VIP Price List** sheet and insert a new row above **row 6**.

16. On the **VIP Price List** sheet enter **VIP Discount** in **cell A6** and enter **15%** in **cell B6**.

17. Save the workbook.

Create Formulas to Calculate Pricing

In this exercise, you will take the Universal Corporate Events price sheet and enter the formulas needed to calculate the new prices for customers.

1. Open **E2-A1-PricesNew** from your **Excel Chapter 2** folder and save it as **E2-A2-PricesNew**.

2. Go to the **Price List** worksheet and enter a formula in **cell C6** that takes the old price for the DJ, band, etc. and adds the Price Increase of 10%. (Hint: Use Old Price+Old Price*Price Increase.)

3. Copy the formula down the column for the other services.

   If the formula was entered correctly in step 2, the prices should all get smaller from top to bottom; however, if some prices are greater than 10,000, then you did not use an absolute reference in step 2, and you will have to go back and correct your formula.

4. Go to the **VIP Price List** sheet and in **cell C7** create the same formula again to add the Price Increase to the Old Price.

5. Enter a new column to the left of *Deposit*.

6. In **cell D4** enter `VIP Price` for the heading.

7. In **cell D7** enter a formula to take the Price and subtract the VIP Discount of 15%. (Hint: Use Price-Price*VIP Discount.)

8. On the **VIP Price List** sheet you can now hide the columns containing Old Price and Price, as well as the rows that contain Price Increase and VIP Discount.

9. On the **Price List** sheet you can hide the Old Price column and Price Increase row.

10. On the **Price List** sheet enter a heading in **cell A14** for a `Total Package Subtotal`.

11. Enter a formula in **cell C14** to find the sum of the prices for all services.

12. After entering the formula in **cell C14**, define a name for the cell and name it `TPackage`.

13. In **cell A15** add the heading `Package Discount`.

14. In **cell C15** enter a formula using the **TPackage** name and multiply by 7%.

15. In **cell A16** enter the heading `Total Package Price`.

16. In **cell C16** enter a formula using the **TPackage** name and multiply by 93%.

17. Select the **range A14:C16**, apply **Bold** format, and then use Format Painter to copy formatting from **row 4** into **row 16**.

18. Apply the **Currency** number format to the **range C14:C16**.

19. Save the workbook and close Excel.

APPLY YOUR SKILLS: E2-A3

Create Formulas Using Names

In this exercise, you will take the Profit and Loss for Universal Corporate Events and use formulas to create projections on a new sheet.

1. Start Excel, open **E2-A3-Profit** from your **Excel Chapter 2** folder, and save it as `E2-A3-ProfitRevised`.

2. Create a copy of **Sheet 1**.

3. Rename the original **Sheet 1** `Profit Q1&Q2` and then rename the copy `Q3&Q4 Projections.`

4. On the **Q3&Q4 Projections** sheet, delete all data in the **range B7:G13**.

5. In **cell A2** add the word `Projections` to the end of the existing text.

6. Edit **cell A3** to `Q3 & Q4`.

7. In **cell A18** enter `Revenue Increase` and in **cell A19** enter `Expense Increase`.

8. In **cell B18** enter `105%` and in **cell B19** enter `103%`.

9. Name **cell B18** `RevIncr` and **cell B19** `ExpIncr`.

10. Hide **rows 18** and **19**, which contain the increases you just entered.

11. Enter the proper headings for **Q3** and **Q4** in **row 5** and the months `Jul` to `Dec` in **row 6**.

12. In **cell B7** use a formula that will take the amount of Revenue from Jan on the **Profit Q1&Q2** sheet and multiply by the **RevIncr** amount, being sure to use the cell name in the formula.

13. Copy the formula across the row for the other months.

14. In **cell B10** enter a formula that will take the amount of Employee Wages from Jan on the **Profit Q1&Q2** sheet and multiply by the **ExpIncr** amount, again being sure to use the cell name in the formula.

15. Copy the formula down the column for the three other expenses and then copy across all six months.

16. Select both the **Profit Q1&Q2** and **Q3&Q4 Projections** sheets and use formulas to calculate Total Expenses in **row 14** for both sheets at once.

17. Apply a **Bottom Border** to the **range B13:H13**.

18. In **row 16** enter a formula to find Profit or Loss for each month. (Hint: Take Revenue–Total Expenses.)

19. Find the Total for Revenue and each Expense as well as Total Expense and Profit/Loss in **column H**.

20. With both sheets still selected, apply **Bold** and **Accounting** number format to all numbers in **column H** and **row 16**.

21. Save the workbook and close Excel.

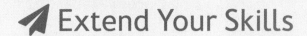 Extend Your Skills

These exercises challenge you to think critically and apply your new skills. You will be evaluated on your ability to follow directions, completeness, creativity, and the use of proper grammar and mechanics. Save files to your chapter folder. Submit assignments as directed.

E2-E1 That's the Way I See It

You are a real estate agent, and you want to create a list comparing potential house purchase costs for your clients. Open **E2-E1-REPurchase** and save it as **E2-E1-REPurchaseRevised**. The purchase costs and the current rate for each are listed, and you need to enter the appropriate formulas. Enter the Price for three houses you might wish to buy, using the Internet, if desired, to research housing prices in your area. Then create formulas in all of the cells with grey shading. Start with the Variable Fees in the top row, multiplying the Price times the Rate and using absolute references so that you can copy the formulas down each column. For the Flat Fees, the formula should just be a reference to the Rate itself. Then use the SUM function to find the Total Fees and add that to the Price to find Total Purchase Cost. When you are done, apply appropriate cell and number formatting as desired. Rename the sheet **Customer 1** and make a copy of it named **Customer 2**. On the **Customer 2** sheet, delete the prices but leave all formulas in place. Save the workbook.

E2-E2 Be Your Own Boss

Information has been gathered from the Blue Jean Landscaping corporate customer invoices for Quarter 1 (Q1), and you need to calculate total Q1 revenue and make revenue projections for Q2. One of your employees has started the file but needs your expertise in creating the formulas. Open **E2-E2-Revenue** and save it as **E2-E2-Projections**. Notice the empty columns, which are where you need to enter your formulas. Use appropriate formulas to calculate Total Labor (Hours times Labor Rate) and the Total Invoice (Materials plus Total Labor). Then you can calculate Q2 projections using the Total Invoice and multiplying by the expected Q2 Growth rate. Also enter formulas to find the Total Invoices and Average Customer Invoice for both Total Invoices and Q2 Projections. Last, you should clean up your worksheet by deleting the companies with 0 material and hours, hide the Labor Rate and Q2 Growth rows, and sort the companies by Total Invoice from smallest to largest. Rename the worksheet **Q1** and make a copy of it named **Q2**. Save the workbook.

E2-E3 Demonstrate Proficiency

After introducing two new flavors of BBQ sauce last year, Stormy BBQ wants you to do an analysis of its sales for each type of sauce and calculate total profit for each. Open **E2-E3-SauceSales**, save it as **E2-E3-SauceSalesRevised**, and begin by defining names for each of the columns of sauce data. (Hint: Select the data for World Famous, January to December, and then create the name using the sauce name.) Once you have named the three ranges, one for each sauce, create headings and then insert the appropriate formulas below December to find the **Total Annual Sales**, **Average Sales**, **Highest Sale Amount**, **and** **Lowest Sale Amount**. Do this for each sauce and use the names you have created in your formulas. Once this is done, unhide row 5 and create a formula to find Total Annual Profit for each sauce; each bottle sells for $7.00. (Hint: Your formula will take the price, subtract the cost, and then multiply by the Total Annual Sales number—be sure to use brackets to ensure the correct order of operations.) Be sure to apply appropriate formatting to Total Annual Profit because this is now a $ figure and then hide row 5 once again. Save the workbook.

3 Data Visualization and Images

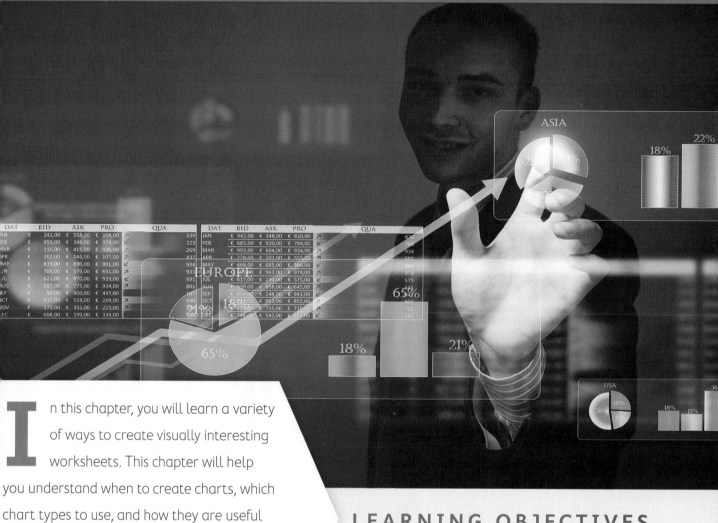

I n this chapter, you will learn a variety of ways to create visually interesting worksheets. This chapter will help you understand when to create charts, which chart types to use, and how they are useful in understanding relationships between numbers in a worksheet. You will also learn about formatting data based on desired conditions and inserting pictures and shapes.

LEARNING OBJECTIVES

▸ Insert charts

▸ Use chart tools to modify charts

▸ Move and size charts

▸ Edit chart data

▸ Add images to a worksheet

▸ Apply conditional formatting

📁 Project: Reporting Company Sales Data

Airspace Travel has put together a report of sales figures for the year and has asked you to help create some charts. You have to decide what data to use to create the charts and the chart types that will best help the company understand how it is performing. You want to show sales comparisons month by month, illustrate the contributions of each travel agent to compare them side by side, and highlight the top and bottom performers throughout the year.

Create Charts to Compare Data

There are many situations in which we are presented with numerical data, and it would be easier to interpret the data if we could visualize it in chart form. Charts are created from worksheet data, and similar to a formula the data is linked so that if the data changes, the chart changes as well. Creating a chart is as easy as selecting the data and chart type, and Excel does the rest. After the chart is created, you can add or modify chart elements to change the way your chart looks.

Choosing a Chart Type

Excel has more than a dozen different types of charts to choose from, with variations of each chart type as well. However, it is important to remember that the purpose of a chart is to simplify data and not make it more complicated. The most common options to use are a column or bar chart, a line chart, or a pie chart.

Column Chart and Bar Chart

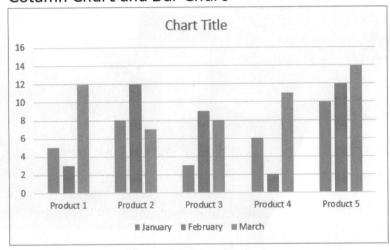

A column chart displays data in columns across the horizontal axis. A bar chart displays data in bars across the vertical axis, so they are basically the same chart, simply vertical up and down or horizontal left to right. Column charts are useful to compare data across several categories.

Line Chart

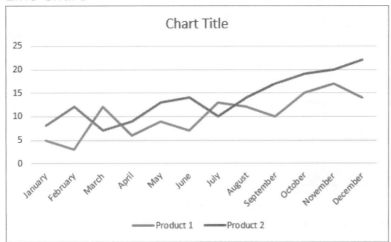

A line chart displays your series of data in a line or several lines and is useful for showing trends in data over time, such as days, months, or years. Line charts are best for a large amount of data and when the order of data, for example chronological, is important. Line charts are very similar to column charts and have most of the same features.

Pie Chart

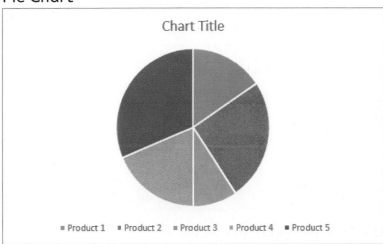

A pie chart shows a comparison of your data as parts of the whole. Pie charts are best for a small amount of data; too many pieces will be hard to see in a pie chart. Pie charts can contain only one series of data, and they do not have a horizontal or vertical axis like column charts and line charts.

Excel also has a Recommended Charts option that will list the top chart options for you based on the data you have selected. The Insert Chart window shows a preview of what your chart will look like before you decide which one to use.

☰ Insert→Charts

☰ Insert→Charts→Recommended Charts 🔱

Selecting Chart Data

Choosing the right data is very important to make sure Excel can create the chart correctly. The best method is to always select the data and include the appropriate row and column headings.

To create a column, bar, or line chart, the data selection is the same.

Q1 Revenue			
	January	February	March
Product 1	1200	1123	1150
Product 2	1301	1235	1260
Product 3	1080	1100	1120
Product 4	1250	1300	1275

The data, including row and column headings, is selected to create your chart; notice the blank cell in the top-left corner is also included.

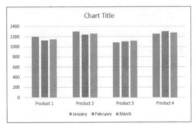 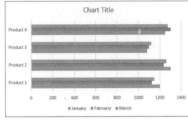 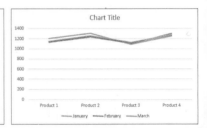

These three charts result from the same selection of data.

To create a pie chart, you can only select one data series.

Q1 Revenue			
	January	February	March
Product 1	1200	1123	1150
Product 2	1301	1235	1260
Product 3	1080	1100	1120
Product 4	1250	1300	1275

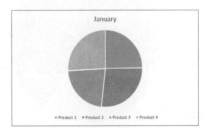

Only the January data series is selected to create the pie chart.

If you want to create charts showing only some of the data, use the [Ctrl] key to select the desired data.

Q1 Revenue			
	January	February	March
Product 1	1200	1123	1150
Product 2	1301	1235	1260
Product 3	1080	1100	1120
Product 4	1250	1300	1275

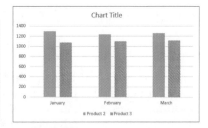

For a column, bar, or line chart showing only Products 2 and 3, you would select the three rows of data as shown, again including the blank cell.

Chart Elements

A chart is made up of different elements that can be added, removed, or modified. These elements can help others understand the information on the chart or accentuate certain aspects of the data. There is a wide range of options for changing the look and style of your chart with each of the chart elements.

Chart area (the whole chart window, where the chart elements are located)

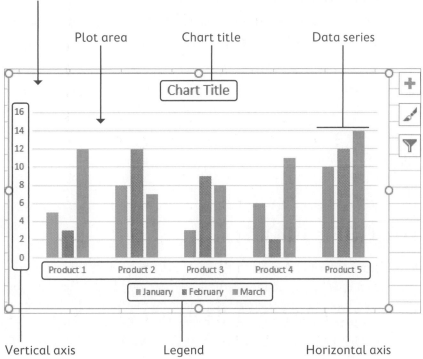

DEVELOP YOUR SKILLS: E3-D1

In this exercise, you will select data and use it to create a chart.

1. Start Excel, open **E3-D1-Sales** from the **Excel Chapter 3** folder, and save it as **E3-D1-SalesCharts**.

2. Follow these steps to insert a column chart:

Ⓐ Select the **range A3:D8** to compare the results for all agents for the first three months of the year.

Ⓑ Choose **Recommended Charts** from the Ribbon.

Ⓒ Excel recommends a clustered column chart. Click **OK** to accept and insert the chart.

Your chart will be inserted as a floating object onto your worksheet, meaning it can be moved easily by dragging.

After creating your chart, notice that resting the mouse pointer over a chart element will display a ScreenTip with the name of the element and pointing to your data will tell you the data series, point, and value.

3. Save the workbook.

Working with Chart Tools

There are countless ways of formatting a chart; your chart can be as simple or as creative as you like. The way you format it will likely depend on your purpose and how much time you want to spend working on it. The Chart Tools are contextual tabs, meaning they are only available while a chart is selected. You can also use the Format pane on the right side of the screen to format chart elements, and the formatting options change for each chart element.

≡ Chart Tools→Format→Current Selection→Format Selection | Right-click→Format (Selection)

Chart Design Tools

You can use Design Tools to quickly and easily change the way your chart looks, using features like Chart Styles and Layouts. Styles modify the colors, shading, and layout of the various chart elements in one easy step. To change the appearance of a chart, there are many other design options, including changing the chart type, changing colors, or adding and removing the various chart elements.

 View the Video "Using the Chart Design Tools."

Using the Chart Formatting Buttons

The chart formatting buttons can add elements to your chart, change the style, or filter the data visible on the chart.

One of the great new features of Excel charts is the ability to filter your data without changing the data selection or creating a new chart. You can simply filter the data to focus on the sets of data you want to compare and then add or remove the other series or categories as desired.

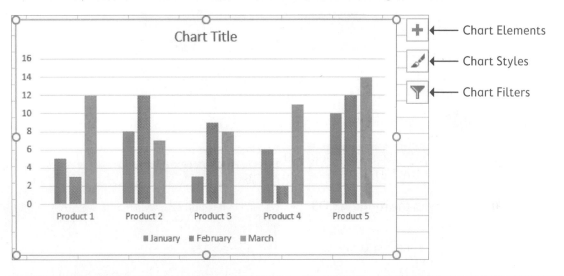

≡ Chart Tools→Design

DEVELOP YOUR SKILLS: E3-D2

In this exercise, you will adjust the appearance of your chart using the style, layout, and other chart design tools.

1. Save your workbook as **E3-D2-SalesCharts**.
2. If necessary, click anywhere on the column chart to select it, which displays the Chart Tools on the Ribbon.
3. Choose **Chart Tools→Design→Chart Styles→Style 8** to apply the new style.
4. Choose **Chart Tools→Design→Chart Layouts→Quick Layout→Layout 1** to apply the layout, which moves the Legend to the right side of the chart.
5. Follow these steps to add axis titles to your chart:

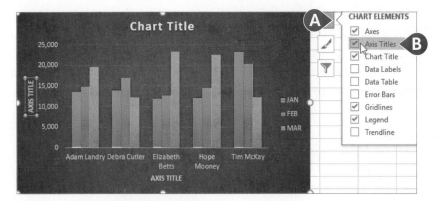

Ⓐ Click on the **Chart Elements** button.

Ⓑ Click to check the box beside **Axis Titles**.

6. Point to the **Vertical Axis Title** you just added and triple-click to select the entire text.

7. Type **Monthly Sales** for the axis title.

8. Select the **Horizontal Axis Title** and replace the text with **Agent** for the title.

9. Replace the **Chart Title** with the title **Airspace Q1 Sales**.

10. Follow these steps to change the chart type:

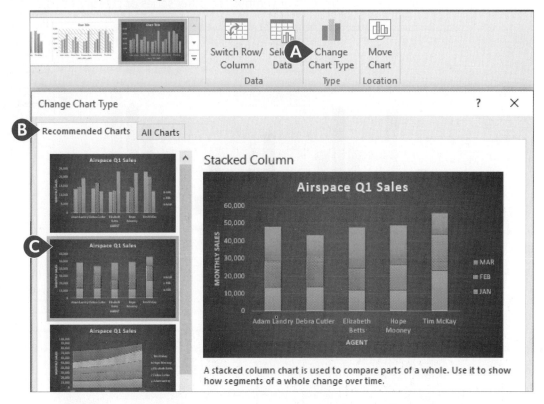

Ⓐ Select **Change Chart Type** from the Ribbon to open the dialog box.

Ⓑ Go to **Recommended Charts**.

Ⓒ Choose the second option, **Stacked Column**, and then click **OK**.

This chart more clearly shows a comparison of the total for each Agent during the three months, as well as the sales for each individual month.

11. Save the workbook.

Chart Format Tools

Beyond changing the basic style of a chart you may want to choose your own colors for the chart area, plot area, or data series. This can be done by modifying the Fill or Outline of a specific chart element. The Fill could be a color, gradient, texture, or even a picture. Other possibilities include adding shapes or WordArt to a chart.

Axis Options

You may want to adjust your axes to focus your data on significant differences or to simply adjust the appearance of the axes. One of the axis options is the minimum and maximum value displayed on the axis. For example, if the data you are charting all falls between 1000 and 1300, you can set your minimum at 1000 to highlight the differences because the first 1000 units are the same for all the data points. Another useful option is to change the Number Format for the axis; for example, to Currency.

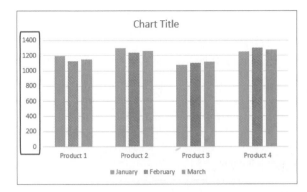

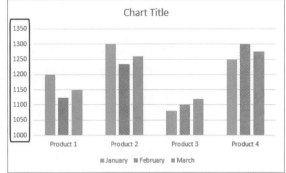

The data looks very similar with the axis values ranging from 0 to 1400.

The Product differences are much easier to see with the axis values starting at 1000.

≡ Chart Tools→Format→Current Selection→Format Selection 🔖 | Right-click axis→Format Axis

---

DEVELOP YOUR SKILLS: E3-D3

In this exercise, you will adjust the chart colors and axis numbering.

1. Save your workbook as **E3-D3-SalesCharts**.

2. Continuing with the **Airspace Q1 Sales** column chart, follow these steps to adjust the color of the FEB series:

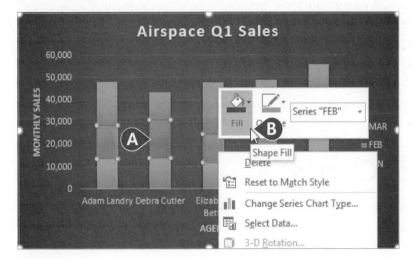

Ⓐ Click once on any orange block to select the FEB Data series.

It is important to click only once. The first click selects the whole series, and clicking a second time would select only one data point from the series to modify.

Ⓑ Right-click, click on **Fill** in the shortcut menu, and then choose **Red** from the Standard Colors.

3. Adjust the Fill Color for the MAR series to **Standard Color Purple**.

4. Follow these steps to adjust the vertical axis:

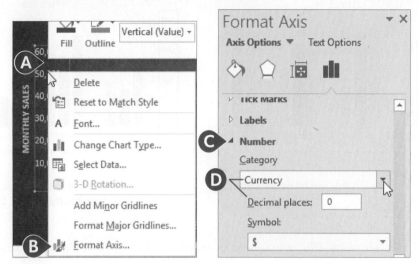

Ⓐ Point to a number on the vertical axis and then right-click to display the shortcut menu.

It is important to point to a number to get the right menu, if you are between the numbers, the Chart Area shortcut menu will appear, which has different options.

Ⓑ Choose the **Format Axis** command.

Ⓒ In the Format Axis pane, scroll to the bottom and click on **Number** to expand (then you may need to scroll down to see Number options).

Ⓓ Choose **Currency** from the Category list using the menu button ▾ and, if necessary, change the Decimal places to **0**.

The Number Format is changed for the vertical axis. You can either leave the Format pane open or close it by clicking the close button in the top-right corner.

5. Save the workbook.

Move and Size Charts

Charts can be moved around on a worksheet or moved to a different worksheet. A chart can be moved on the same sheet by a simple drag, but be sure you click the chart area and not another chart element, or you will be moving that element.

Because charts take up a lot of space, and you may want more than one chart in your workbook, it's often a good idea to move charts onto a separate sheet. Charts that are moved onto their own sheet are referred to as Chart Sheets because they don't contain any rows, columns, or cells—just the chart itself.

To resize a chart, the chart must first be selected. Then you can drag any of the sizing handles to resize appropriately. You can also resize the chart from the Ribbon to specify the exact height and width. Charts on a chart sheet, however, can't be resized.

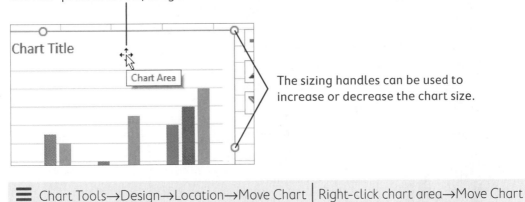

The mouse pointer over the chart area displays the four-pointed arrow; drag to move the chart.

Chart Title

Chart Area

The sizing handles can be used to increase or decrease the chart size.

≡ Chart Tools→Design→Location→Move Chart │ Right-click chart area→Move Chart

≡ Chart Tools→Format→Size

DEVELOP YOUR SKILLS: E3-D4

In this exercise, you will move the existing chart, create another chart, and resize it.

1. Save your workbook as **E3-D4-SalesCharts**.
2. With the **Airspace Q1 Sales** chart selected, choose **Chart Tools→Design→Location→Move Chart** to open the Move Chart dialog box.

   The chart must be selected to display the Chart Tools on the Ribbon.
3. In the dialog box choose **New Sheet**, in the New Sheet box type **Q1 Sales** for the name of the new sheet, and then click **OK**.

   This moves the chart to a chart sheet, which has no cells, and resizes the chart to fit your screen.
4. Go to the **Sales** worksheet to create a new chart.
5. Select the **range A3:G6**, which holds the data for Adam, Debra, and Elizabeth.
6. Choose **Insert→Charts→Insert Line or Area Chart** 📊 **menu button** ▼→**Line** (the first option on the top row in the 2-D Line group).
7. Drag the chart so it is directly below the data.
8. Rename the Chart Title **Semiannual Sales**.
9. Save the workbook.

Edit Chart Data

After a chart has been created, the data is linked, so that if you change the data in the worksheet source, the chart is automatically updated. You can also add or remove data from the chart or filter the chart to change which data is displayed. The easiest way to change the chart data is to reselect the entire range to be used, but you can also add or remove individual data series, points, or labels. You can also modify your chart data by swapping the Horizontal Axis and the Legend categories using the Switch Row/Column button.

EXCEL

Sometimes a better option is to keep all existing data in the chart but use a filter to display only the data you want to see. The Chart Filters feature allows you to quickly filter specific series and category values and then remove the filter later to display all the data again.

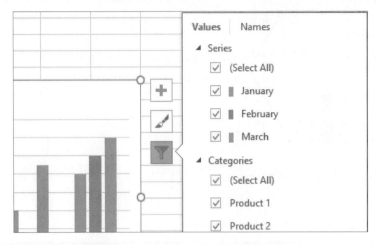

The Chart Filter feature lets you check off the Series or Category you wish to display and uncheck the ones to hide.

☰ Chart Tools→Design→Data→Select Data

☰ Chart Tools→Design→Data→Switch Row/Column

DEVELOP YOUR SKILLS: E3-D5

In this exercise, you will edit the chart to include all five Sales Agents and then filter the data in the chart.

1. Save your workbook as **E3-D5-SalesCharts**.
2. Ensure the **Semiannual Sales** chart is selected on the **Sales** worksheet.
3. Right-click anywhere in the chart and choose **Select Data**.

   The Select Data Source dialog box appears, and the current data has an animated border around it on the worksheet.

4. The Chart data range is already selected, so drag across the worksheet **range A3:G8** to select the new data and click **OK**.

   The new data displays five lines, one for each of the five agents.

5. Click the **Chart Filters** 🔽 button; click the checkbox next to **Adam**, **Elizabeth**, and **Tim** to remove the check and filter out their data; and then click **Apply**.

   You should now see only Debra and Hope's data on the chart and only their names in the legend.

6. Adjust the Number format for the vertical axis to display **Currency** with no decimals.
7. Save the workbook.

Add Images to a Worksheet

For the most part Excel is used for text and data; however, it is also possible to add pictures and shapes to a worksheet. Pictures might be used to display a company logo, add information to a spreadsheet, or simply add a little excitement to an otherwise plain set of data. Pictures can be added from your computer or from an online search, and many types of shapes can be added via the menu button.

Adding a picture lets you access the Picture Tools features on the Ribbon, and adding a shape allows you to access the Drawing Tools. Both of these contextual tabs give you a great number of options for changing the style, shape, color, and size and for modifying many other aspects of the image as well.

Allows you to add pictures you have already saved on your computer ———→

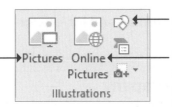

Accesses the shapes library here; browse to find the desired shape and click to add it

Will insert pictures from OneDrive or Bing, a web search engine from Microsoft that lets you browse an endless supply of images from the Internet

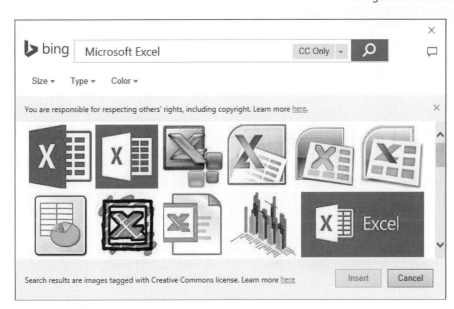

Using Online Pictures to do a Bing Search for Microsoft Excel returns many variations of the Excel logo.

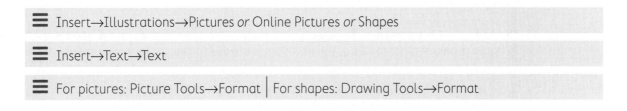

☰ Insert→Illustrations→Pictures *or* Online Pictures *or* Shapes

☰ Insert→Text→Text

☰ For pictures: Picture Tools→Format | For shapes: Drawing Tools→Format

---

DEVELOP YOUR SKILLS: E3-D6

In this exercise, you will add a picture to the worksheet and make some modifications.

1. Save your workbook as **E3-D6-SalesCharts**.
2. Select **cell J1** on the **Sales** sheet and then choose **Insert→Illustrations→Online Pictures** 🖼 to open the dialog box.

3. Search for **air travel** in the Bing Search, choose a suitable image with a plane, and then click **Insert**.

   Because this is an online search, the results will frequently change, and you may not see the same images from one search to the next.

4. With the image selected, go to **Picture Tools→Format→Size→Height** ⬍, type **1** in the box, and then tap Enter .

5. Select **cell I1** and choose **Insert→Illustrations→Online Pictures** 🖼 again.

6. Search for **space** in the Bing Search, choose an appropriate image of a spaceship, and then click **Insert**.

7. Resize this image to be **1"** in height to match the first image.

8. Choose **Picture Tools→Format→Adjust→Color→Blue, Accent color 1 Light** (in the Recolor group).

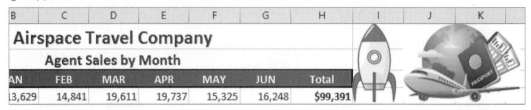

B	C	D	E	F	G	H	I	J	K
Airspace Travel Company									
Agent Sales by Month									
AN	FEB	MAR	APR	MAY	JUN	Total			
3,629	14,841	19,611	19,737	15,325	16,248	$99,391			

9. Save the workbook.

Use Conditional Formatting

 View the video "Highlighting Data with Conditional Formatting."

Another way to better visualize your data is to use conditional formatting. Conditional formatting takes a set of data, applies a rule or rules, and modifies the formatting of the cells that match the rule. For example, you may have a large set of data containing student grades and want to quickly find the top three marks in the class. Or you may have sales data for a group of products and want to find which product sells the most and which one sells the least. Conditional formatting applies formatting of your choice to the cells that meet these criteria so that you can quickly find them.

Rules can be created to draw attention to the top, or bottom, or to numbers greater than or less than a specific number. You can also highlight a cell with a number equal to a specific amount or a cell that contains certain text; there are so many options!

To apply conditional formatting, the first step is always to select the entire range of data to apply the rule to. For conditional formatting, unlike with charts, you do not include any labels and generally don't include any totals unless you set up a separate rule for total rows or columns. Different rule options are available from the Conditional Formatting drop-down menu, but the criteria and formatting can also be modified to suit your needs. After a rule has been created, you can Clear Rules or Manage Rules to see all existing rules for either the current selection or the entire worksheet.

◢	A	B	C	D
1		January	February	March
2	Product 1	5	3	12
3	Product 2	8	12	7
4	Product 3	3	9	8
5	Product 4	6	2	11
6	Product 5	10	12	14

◢	A	B	C	D
1		January	February	March
2	Product 1	5	3	12
3	Product 2	8	12	7
4	Product 3	3	9	8
5	Product 4	6	2	11
6	Product 5	10	12	14

The worksheet before creating conditional formatting, with the range selected

The worksheet after the conditional formatting rule is applied to the range, highlighting the top five items with Light Red Fill and Dark Red Text

 Note! *When a conditional formatting rule is created for the top five items, if two or more items are tied for fifth highest, six or more items could be included in the conditional formatting.*

After a conditional formatting rule is created, if the data changes, the formatting is automatically updated to reflect the new data.

≡ Home→Styles→Conditional Formatting 📊

DEVELOP YOUR SKILLS: E3-D7

In this exercise, you will alter the appearance of the data using conditional formatting to show some of the top and bottom sales numbers for the agents.

1. Save your workbook as **E3-D7-SalesCharts**.

2. Select the **range B4:G8** and choose **Home→Styles→Conditional Formatting** 📊 **→ Highlight Cells Rules**.

3. Choose **Greater Than**, and then in the dialog box that opens, adjust the GREATER THAN value to **20000** (that is 20,000, with no comma needed).

   The preview shows which data this will apply to.

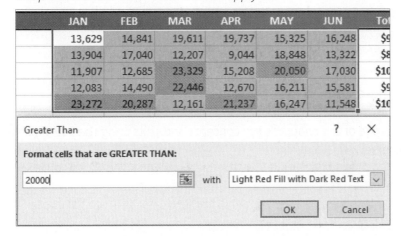

4. Click **OK** to apply the format and close the dialog box.

   For the six-month total you want to see the top and bottom agents, so you will apply two new rules to the data in column H under Total.

5. Select the **range H4:H8** and choose **Home→Styles→Conditional Formatting→Top/Bottom Rules→Top 10 Items**.

6. Change the *10* to **1**, change the format to **Green Fill with Dark Green Text**, and click **OK**.

7. With the **range H4:H8** still selected, choose **Home→Styles→Conditional Formatting→Top/Bottom Rules→Bottom 10 Items**.

8. Change the *10* to **1**, change the format to **Yellow Fill with Dark Yellow Text**, and click **OK**.

   Now the data needs to be updated. A sale was missed for Debra in March, so the number should be higher.

9. Select **cell D5** and edit the number *12,207* to be **22,207**.

   Notice that the formatting for cell D7 changes to red fill and red text, the formatting in the Total column also changes because Debra is no longer the lowest Total, and your Semiannual Sales chart below the data updates as well. Your worksheet should now look like this.

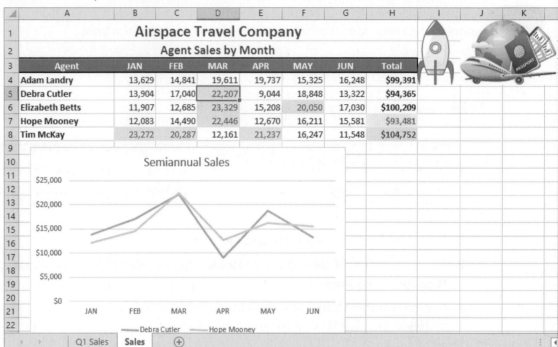

10. Save the workbook.

Self-Assessment

 Check your knowledge of this chapter's key concepts and skills using the Self-Assessment in your ebook or eLab course.

REINFORCE YOUR SKILLS: E3-R1

Create and Modify Charts

In this exercise, you will create several charts to compare volunteer hours for the Kids for Change volunteers and then make some changes to the charts.

1. Start Excel, open **E3-R1-VHours** from your **Excel Chapter 3** folder, and save it as **E3-R1-VHoursSummary**.

2. Select the **ranges A4:A10** and **N4:N10**.

   Remember to use the Ctrl *button to select nonadjacent ranges.*

3. Choose **Insert→Charts→Recommended Charts** ⏺.

4. Select the third option, the **Pie** chart, then click **OK**.

5. Edit the Chart Title from *Total* to **Annual Total**.

6. Move the chart to its own sheet and name the new sheet **Hours by Volunteer**.

7. Return to the **Summary** sheet and select the **ranges A4:M4** and **A11:M11**.

8. Choose **Insert→Charts→Insert Line or Area Chart** ⏺ **menu button** ▾→**3-D Area** (the first option on the bottom row in the 3-D Area group).

9. Edit the Chart Title from *Total* to **Monthly Total**.

10. Click the **Chart Elements** ⊞ button.

11. Place your mouse over Axes and then click the **menu** button ▸ that appears beside **Axes** to expand the options.

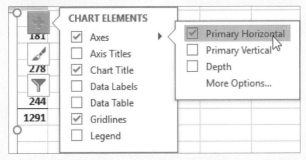

12. Uncheck the box beside **Primary Vertical** and **Depth** to remove those axes from the chart.

13. Right-click the data series and change the Fill to a **Texture→Purple Mesh**.

14. Modify the Chart Area Fill to **Blue-Gray, Text 2, Darker 50%** (under Theme Colors).

15. Move the chart to its own sheet and name the new sheet **Hours by Month**.

16. Go to the **Hours by Volunteer** sheet and change the Annual Total chart type from a Pie Chart to a **3-D Clustered Bar**.

17. Change the Layout to **Layout 5**, which includes a data table below the chart.

18. Save the workbook.

Format Charts and Add Conditional Formatting

In this exercise, you will make some further changes to your charts and then add conditional formatting rules to your data.

1. Save your workbook as **E3-R2-VHoursSummary**.
2. Go to the **Hours by Month** sheet and select the **Horizontal Axis**.
3. Increase the Font Size to **12** and then right-click and choose **Format Axis**.
4. Click to select **Text Options**. If necessary, expand the Text Fill options and then change the Color to **White, Background 1**.
5. Leave the Format Pane open, select the **Chart Title**, and change the Text Fill to **White, Background 1**, and then close the Format Pane.
6. Use the **Chart Filters** button to remove the first six months from the chart, leaving only the data for July to December.
7. Go back to the **Summary** worksheet and select the **range B5:M10**.
8. Apply a Conditional Formatting Rule to Highlight Cells that are Greater than **29** with **Light Red Fill and Dark Red Text**.
9. Select the **range N5:N10**.
10. Apply a Conditional Formatting Rule to show the top three cells with **Green Fill and Dark Green Text**.
11. Select the **range B11:M11**.
12. Apply a Conditional Formatting Rule to show the top three cells with **Green Fill and Dark Green Text**.
13. Save the workbook and close Excel.

Add Visual Aids for a Financial Summary

In this exercise, you will use data from the Kids for Change Summer Fundraising results and will create charts, edit charts, add pictures, and use conditional formatting.

1. Start Excel, open **E3-R3-SummerFunds** from your **Excel Chapter 3** folder, and save it as **E3-R3-SummerFundsResults**.

2. Select the **range A4:D8**.

3. Insert a **2-D Clustered Column** chart.

4. Change the Chart Style to **Style 8**.

5. Modify the Chart Area by changing the Fill to **Dark Blue**.

6. Change the June Series Fill to **Purple**, and for the July Series change the Fill to **White, Background 1**.

7. Change the Chart Title to **Results**.

8. Move the chart to a new sheet named **Results**.

9. Go back to the **Summary** sheet and select the **ranges B4:D4** and **B9:D9**.

10. Insert a **3-D Pie** chart and then remove the title and the legend elements from the chart.

11. Move the chart as an object to the **Results** sheet.

12. Remove the Chart Area Fill from the Pie Chart you just moved (choose **Fill** and then **No Fill**) and then remove the Outline in the same way.

13. Change the June Series Fill to **Purple**, and for the July Series change the Fill to **White, Background 1**.

14. Move the Pie Chart to the top-right corner of the column chart and change the size to **2.5"** tall.

15. Edit the vertical axis to be **Currency with no decimal places**, **Bold**, and in **10** pt font size.

16. Edit the horizontal axis to also be **Bold** and **10** pt font size.

17. Increase the Title to **20** pt font size.

18. Go back to the summary sheet and create a conditional formatting rule that will apply red text to the top three numbers in the **range B5:D8**.

19. Search for Online Pictures of *running* and *barbecue* and insert the images below the Total in **cell A9**.

20. Resize both images to **0.75"** tall.

21. Save the workbook and close Excel.

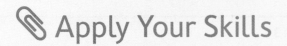 Apply Your Skills

Create Charts and Use Chart Tools

In this exercise, you will use the expense data and revenue data for Universal Corporate Events to create two charts and then edit the charts.

1. Start Excel, open **E3-A1-Profit** from your **Excel Chapter 3** folder, and save it as **E3-A1-ProfitSummary**.
2. Go to the **Profit Q1&Q2** sheet.
3. Select the **ranges A6:G6** and **A10:G13** and then insert a **2-D Clustered Column** chart.
4. Change the chart layout to **Layout 11**.
5. Choose **Chart Tools→Design→Data→Switch Row/Column** to switch the Months to the Legend and the categories to the Horizontal Axis.
6. Choose **Chart Tools→Design→Chart Styles→Change Colors→Monochromatic Palette 8** to make all series different shades of blue.
7. Change the Chart Style to **Style 8**.
8. Move the chart to a new sheet and name the sheet **Expenses**.
9. Go back to the **Profit Q1&Q2** sheet and select the **range A6:G7**.
10. Insert a **2-D line** chart and adjust the style and colors to **Monochromatic Color 8** and **Style 7**.
11. Move the chart to a new sheet and name the sheet **Revenue**.
12. Adjust the vertical axis format to display the Minimum value as **15,000** rather than zero.
13. Remove the Chart Title from the **Revenue** chart.
14. Save the workbook.

Apply Conditional Formatting Rules

In this exercise, you will use conditional formatting rules to identify the month with the highest revenue or expense for each category.

1. Save your workbook as **E3-A2-ProfitSummary**.
2. If necessary, go to the **Profit Q1&Q2** sheet.
3. Select the **range B7:G7** (the six months of data in row 7 for Revenue); do not include the total.
4. Create a conditional formatting rule to format the TOP 1 cell with **Red Text**.
5. Select the cells with the six months of data in row 10 for Employee Wages and again create a conditional formatting rule to format the TOP 1 cell with **Red Text**.

   Notice that because the numbers are identical, the formatting applies to all of them.
6. Repeat this process again, five separate times, one time for each of the rows of data for Capital Expenditures, Material Costs, Marketing & Sales, Total Expenses, and Profit/Loss.
7. Select **cell D17** and insert a picture of an **up arrow** using an Online Picture.

8. Resize the inserted picture to **1"** tall.

9. Save the workbook and close Excel.

APPLY YOUR SKILLS: E3-A3

Create Visual Tools for a Financial Forecast

In this exercise, you will create and modify a chart displaying the long-term financial forecast for Universal Corporate Events.

1. Start Excel, open **E3-A3-LTForecast** from your **Excel Chapter 3** folder, and save it as **E3-A3-5yrForecast**.

2. Create a **3-D Column** chart using the data from Revenue and Expenses for all five years. (Be sure to include the year headings.)

3. Change the Fill for Revenue to **Gold, Accent 4** and the Fill for Expenses to **Standard Dark Red**.

4. Remove the Chart Title completely.

5. Move the chart so it is directly below Profit/Loss in **row 8** and roughly centered below the data.

6. Edit the Chart Data to include Profit/Loss in **row 8**.

7. Change the Chart Type to a **Combo Chart**, with Revenue and Total Expenses being a Clustered Column Chart Type and Profit/Loss being a Line Chart.

8. Modify the Outline for Profit/Loss to **Standard Dark Blue.**

9. Edit the Number Format for the Vertical Axis to be **Currency** format with no decimals.

10. Create a Conditional Formatting rule to show the Profit/Loss cells that are greater than **$100,000** with **Yellow Fill** and **Dark Yellow Text**.

11. Insert the **UniversalCorporateEvents.jpg** logo file from the **Excel Chapter 3** folder in **cell E1** to the right of the sheet title and resize the logo to **1"** tall.

12. Save the workbook and close Excel.

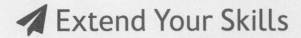 Extend Your Skills

These exercises challenge you to think critically and apply your new skills. You will be evaluated on your ability to follow directions, completeness, creativity, and the use of proper grammar and mechanics. Save files to your chapter folder. Submit assignments as directed.

E3-E1   That's the Way I See It

As a student who prides yourself on achieving top grades, you want to create a chart of your achievements. Create a new blank worksheet and set up headings so that you can list your recent classes in one column and the grades for those classes in the next. List your classes in chronological order, oldest to newest (at least 10 classes), and then insert your grades in the next column (if you don't have access to your grades, just make up numbers). Create a line chart from the data to show the trend in grades over time. Modify the chart to use your favorite colors and use conditional formatting to highlight the top three grades and the lowest three grades you received. Save your workbook as **E3-E1-ClassGrades**.

E3-E2   Be Your Own Boss

You are looking to acquire more funding to expand Blue Jean Landscaping after a very successful year. You are preparing a report on last year's financial statements, and you want to include some charts to emphasize your revenue growth and expense reduction. Open **E3-E2-RevandExp**, select the data, and then choose the best chart to show this trend. Insert the **BlueJeanLandscaping.jpg** logo and modify the chart as you see fit so that it looks professional and presentable. Apply conditional formatting to highlight the top three Revenue months and the bottom three Expense months. Save your workbook as **E3-E2-RevandExpCharts**.

E3-E3   Demonstrate Proficiency

The BBQ sauce sales were very encouraging for their two new flavors last year, and Stormy BBQ has asked you to create some charts that represent a comparison of its three sauces. Open the file **E3-E3-SauceSales** and use the data to create both a column chart and a line chart for the year. Move both of these charts to new sheets. Then add a total at the bottom for each sauce and create a pie chart comparing the three totals. Be sure to include the Stormy BBQ logo (**StormyBBQ.jpg**) on each chart and adjust the styles, layouts, and formatting in the charts appropriately. Try and use the corporate colors, red and gold, where possible. Save your workbook as **E3-E3-SauceSalesCharts**.

4 Organizing Large Amounts of Data

I n this chapter, you will learn about managing large amounts of data and how to utilize different sources of data. You will learn some of the more advanced Excel tools used for organizing data, performing calculations, and restricting data entry.

LEARNING OBJECTIVES

▸ Start a workbook from a template

▸ Import and export data

▸ Change worksheet view options

▸ Sort and filter data

▸ Create IF functions

▸ Apply data validation rules

▸ Use the Scale to Fit options

▸ Create and modify tables

Project: Preparing Company Payroll Data

Every two weeks, Airspace Travel goes through the process of compiling the data from hours worked and commissions earned to calculate employee paychecks. You have been asked to take over, which means taking the data and importing it into a template and then inserting the required formulas into the sheet that will calculate gross pay. You will also need to organize the data so it is presentable, easy to read, and easy to print if necessary.

Starting with a Template

Using templates in Excel is a way to save yourself a lot of work. Templates allow you to use a preexisting workbook, which usually has the formatting, headings, and certain other aspects of the workbook already created for you. Excel offers a large collection of online templates, which you can search through to find something suitable for your purpose.

Another option is to create your own template. Creating your own template means creating a workbook and inserting the headings and format you desire but not filling in any actual data. Then when you save the workbook, you change the type of file to an Excel Template.

The default file type when saving your work is Excel Workbook, which can be changed to Excel Template.

When you start Excel, you have the option of either opening a workbook, starting a Blank Workbook, or using a template.

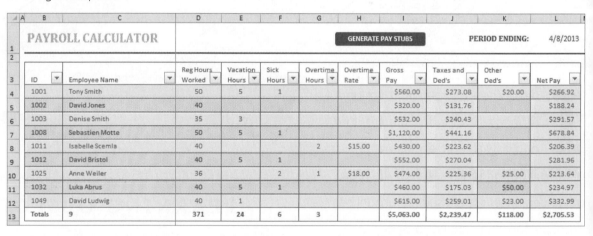

ID	Employee Name	Reg Hours Worked	Vacation Hours	Sick Hours	Overtime Hours	Overtime Rate	Gross Pay	Taxes and Ded's	Other Ded's	Net Pay
1001	Tony Smith	50	5	1			$560.00	$273.08	$20.00	$266.92
1002	David Jones	40					$320.00	$131.76		$188.24
1003	Denise Smith	35	3				$532.00	$240.43		$291.57
1008	Sebastien Motte	50	5	1			$1,120.00	$441.16		$678.84
1011	Isabelle Scemla	40			2	$15.00	$430.00	$223.62		$206.39
1012	David Bristol	40	5	1			$552.00	$270.04		$281.96
1025	Anne Weiler	36		2	1	$18.00	$474.00	$225.36	$25.00	$223.64
1032	Luka Abrus	40	5	1			$460.00	$175.03	$50.00	$234.97
1049	David Ludwig	40	1				$615.00	$259.01	$23.00	$332.99
Totals	9	371	24	6	3		$5,063.00	$2,239.47	$118.00	$2,705.53

An example of a template used for payroll calculations already has the structure, formatting, and formulas in place; however, be aware that some templates require users to have advanced Excel knowledge.

In this exercise, you will start Excel, browse templates, and start a new workbook from a template.

1. Start Excel.

   Notice the FEATURED list of options for you. The first is the Blank Workbook, and then there are several feature tours, followed by a list of template options you can scroll down and browse through.

2. Go to Search for Online Templates at the top of the screen, click inside the box, and type **Payroll**. Then tap Enter .

   It may take a moment or two to search through thousands of online templates and then a list of potential templates appears. If you like, you can click on an option to preview or open up a template to look at it. Airspace Travel has already created a template for you to use, so you will open that template now.

3. Close Excel and use File Explorer to open **E4-D1-PayrollTemplate** from your **Excel Chapter 4** folder.

   Notice that a 1 has been added to the end of the filename in the title bar, similar to when you create a new blank workbook and the default name is Book1.

4. Use **Save As** to save the workbook as **E4-D1-PayrollP17**.

   Now that it has been saved, this is just a regular Excel file for you to work on, and the template remains unchanged for future use.

Importing and Exporting Data

Excel is certainly a very useful program, but companies use many other programs for a variety of business-related tasks. This means that data needs to be transferable between programs that are used for different purposes; for example, a business might use accounting software to perform certain bookkeeping tasks and then use the financial data from the accounting software in Excel to create financial forecasts.

To accomplish this, data can be saved in one of several common formats that most programs understand. Doing this allows you to import and export data in and out of various programs that are otherwise incompatible. One of the more common file formats for importing and exporting data is the CSV (*.csv*) format, which stands for comma separated values. Data in a CSV file typically comes from a database, which has text and numerical data entered in fields, and each field is then separated by a comma.

Characters such as the comma, space, or tab can be used as delimiters, which are any character used to specify a boundary between separate regions (also called fields) when working with data. You can use CSV files to import and export data between Word, Excel, Access, and many more programs, including most accounting and database software.

In Excel, any file can be saved as a CSV version from the *Save as Type* option in the *Save As* window. Other popular formats in which to save an Excel file include PDF, for a read-only file, and HTML, to create a web page. To import data into Excel from another source, there is an Import Wizard that walks you through the process in just a few steps.

≡ File→Save As→Save as Type

≡ Data→Get External Data

DEVELOP YOUR SKILLS: E4-D2

In this exercise, you will import the payroll data for this period into Excel.

1. Save your workbook as **E4-D2-PayrollP17**.

2. Click to select **cell A6**, if necessary.

   Cell A6 is the target location where you want to import the data, and although this can be changed later, you can make it easier on yourself by selecting the proper cell now.

3. Choose **Data→Get External Data→From Text** 🗋.

4. Navigate to the **Excel Chapter 4** folder, select the **E4-D2-PayrollPeriod17data** CSV file, and then click **Import**.

   This launches the Text Import Wizard, which will assist you.

   The first step allows you to choose the data type, Delimited or Fixed Width, and gives you a preview. The delimited option is already selected, which is correct because the fields are separated by commas.

5. Click **Next**.

   The second step asks you what Delimiter is used in the file you are importing and again gives you a preview.

6. Click the checkbox next to **Comma**.

   Using the placement of the commas in the CSV file, Excel will determine how to divide the data into columns and rows in Excel; you can see in the preview how the data is now separated into columns.

7. Click **Next**.

   The last step allows you to adjust the data format for each column. The General format keeps numbers as numbers, dates as dates, and everything else as text, which is correct for all columns to be imported.

8. Click **Finish**.

   The data is ready to be imported into the Existing worksheet. You already selected the desired target location, cell A6, but you could also adjust it now, if necessary.

9. Ensure **cell A6** is the cell where the data will be placed and click **OK**.

10. Set the following columns to the listed column widths so that the full headings can be seen.

Heading	Width
Employee ID#	9
Hours	6
Rate	6
Commissions	12

11. In **cell A3** add the pay period number so the cell reads **Period: 17**.

12. Save the workbook.

Adjust View Options for Large Worksheets

When you have large amounts of data, it can be difficult to see it all and do what you need to do. When you scroll down, you will no longer see your headings, so you can also lose track of what information is in each column, or you might want to see different parts of a spreadsheet at the same time for comparison. Using different view options can help make it easier to work with these large worksheets.

Freeze Panes

To keep the headings of your worksheet visible while you scroll down or across through your data, you can use the Freeze Panes feature. You can Unfreeze the panes again at any time.

If cell B5 is selected, this option would freeze column A *and* rows 1:4, so the Inventory ID and all column headings would always remain visible.

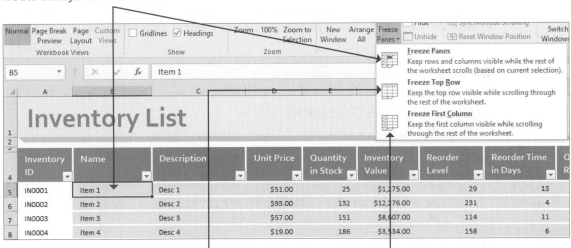

This option freezes row 1 only.

This freezes column A only; you cannot use Freeze Top Row and Freeze First Column at the same time.

≡ View→Window→Freeze Panes ⊞

Split a Window

Another option is to Split a window, either into two halves or four quadrants. This allows you to scroll through different areas of your worksheet in the different split views, which would be useful if you need to refer back and forth to data from different sections of your worksheet. Similar to Freeze Panes, the location of the Split is based on the current active cell. To divide your worksheet in two halves, simply choose a cell in column A before creating the split. You can remove the Split at any time.

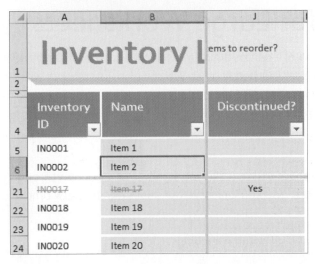

The split lines shown here divide the worksheet into four quadrants, and each can be scrolled through separately to view four different areas of the worksheet.

☰ View→Window→Split

Change the Workbook View

Another issue with large worksheets is understanding how your worksheet will look when it is printed. To see how your worksheet will look when printed, or to see where the page breaks will occur, you can use the Page Break Preview or Page Layout view.

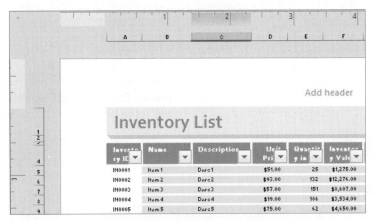

Page Layout view shows the ruler and allows you to view and edit the margins and header and footer sections.

☰ View→Workbook Views

DEVELOP YOUR SKILLS: E4-D3

In this exercise, you will make adjustments to view the worksheet several different ways.

1. Save your workbook as **E4-D3-PayrollP17**.

2. Select **cell C6** and then choose **View→Window→Split** 🔲.

   Use the scroll bars and mouse wheel to scroll through the worksheet in each of the four quadrants.

3. Turn off the split by choosing **View→Window→Split** 🔲 a second time.

4. Scroll back to the top left of your worksheet if you are not already there.

5. Select **cell C6** again, and this time choose **View→Window→Freeze Panes** 🔲 **→Freeze Panes**.

   Use the scroll bars and mouse wheel to scroll through the worksheet up and down, left and right. Notice that the headings and employee names remain visible.

6. Change the view by choosing **View→Workbook Views→Page Layout** 📄.

   Because Page Layout View isn't compatible with Freeze Panes, it will automatically unfreeze the panes.

7. Click **OK** to continue.

   Notice the Status Bar at the bottom now displays the number of pages in your document. You can scroll down to view the second page.

8. Switch back to the **Normal** ▦ view.

9. Save the workbook.

Sort and Filter to Organize Data

When you have large amounts of data, you need tools to help you make sense of it. Sorting gives you the ability to rearrange your data in the way that makes the most sense for your purpose. Filtering then allows you to narrow down your data to focus on certain parts of it.

Sort Data

Sorting can be performed on any column, using text values, numerical values, or even cell color or font color. Values can be sorted A to Z or Z to A for text, and smallest to largest or largest to smallest for numbers. You can also add multiple levels to your sorting; for example, you might have an employee database with information like department, job titles, location, sales performance, and how long employees have been with the company, and you might decide to sort the data based on department first and then by length of time with the company.

Filter Data

Filtering allows you to choose what data to include and what data to filter out. You can also filter by text or numbers. For text you can create many filters to find data; for example, to find text that begins with or ends with a letter or that contains a certain string of text. For numeric values there are also numerous different ways to create rules to find values that are greater than, less than, equal to, and so on. Using the same company example, you could filter the list multiple ways to view only employees in the sales department, with five or more years of experience, and with less than $10,000 in sales last month.

A customer list with no sort or filter applied	A customer list sorted by Country and then by Customers	A customer list filtered to show only customers in the USA

Customers	Country
Carol Gregory	USA
Natasha Dyas	Canada
James Norman	Mexico
Joshua Garcia	USA
Sarah Mckinnon	USA
Shannon Miller	Mexico
Katrina Kormylo	Canada
Susan Colley	USA
William Emerson	Canada
Eugene Fink	USA

Customers	Country
Katrina Kormylo	Canada
Natasha Dyas	Canada
William Emerson	Canada
James Norman	Mexico
Shannon Miller	Mexico
Carol Gregory	USA
Eugene Fink	USA
Joshua Garcia	USA
Sarah Mckinnon	USA
Susan Colley	USA

Customers ▼	Country ▼
Carol Gregory	USA
Eugene Fink	USA
Joshua Garcia	USA
Sarah Mckinnon	USA
Susan Colley	USA

 View the video "Using Sort and Filter."

☰ Data→Sort & Filter→Sort

☰ Data→Sort & Filter→Filter

DEVELOP YOUR SKILLS: E4-D4

In this exercise, you will use Sort & Filter to organize the employee data and edit the Rate for some of the employees.

1. Save your workbook as **E4-D4-PayrollP17**.
2. Select any cell that contains data within the **range A6:H63**.

3. Choose **Data→Sort & Filter→Sort** 🔲.

   Notice that Excel automatically selects the entire range of adjacent data to sort, which is easier than trying to select the entire range yourself.

4. Follow these steps to sort the data with multiple levels:

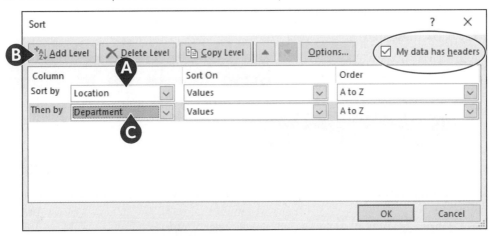

Ⓐ Choose **Sort by Location**.

   Excel recognizes your data has headers in the top row, so you can select the name of the column you wish to sort by from the drop-down menu; without headers the menu would show only Column A, Column B, etc.

Ⓑ Click **Add Level** to perform an additional sort.

Ⓒ Choose **Then by Department** and then click **OK**.

Your data will now be sorted, with Los Angeles employees listed at the top and Vancouver employees listed at the bottom. Within each location the employees will be sorted by Department, as shown below.

First Name	Last Name	Employee ID#	Location	Department
Jasmin	Newton	13651	Los Angeles	Administration
Tim	Parker	17232	Los Angeles	Administration
Carol	Gregory	16688	Los Angeles	Management
Kobe	Curry	20303	Los Angeles	Sales
Tracy	Bryant	14917	Los Angeles	Sales
Cam	Owens	22404	Los Angeles	Sales
Ashley	Bradford	17571	Miami	Administration
Deborah	Secrett	16735	Miami	Administration
Adel	Kahlmeier	13089	Miami	Administration
Brett	Aberle	22113	Miami	Administration
Tony	Duncan	12743	Miami	Administration
James	Norman	13733	Miami	Management
Melissa	Coelho	21635	Miami	Management
Sophia	Maria	13365	Miami	Management
Steven	Samuel	15563	Miami	Sales

Now you can filter your data to narrow it down.

5. Ensure once again that you have a cell selected within the sorted list.

Remember you need only a single cell selected anywhere within the range of data you wish to sort or filter; Excel will automatically detect the correct range.

6. Choose **Data→Sort & Filter→Filter** ▼.

Notice the menu buttons that appear beside all of your column headings.

7. Follow these steps to filter your data:

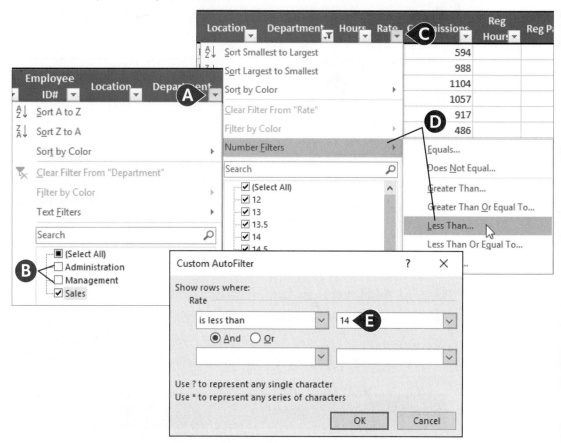

Ⓐ Click the **Department menu** button ▼.

Ⓑ Filter the Department column to include only Sales employees by removing the checks next to **Administration** and **Management** and then click **OK**.

Ⓒ Click the **Rate menu** button ▼.

Ⓓ Choose **Number Filters→Less Than** to open the dialog box.

Ⓔ Type **14** to the right of *Show Rows Where Rate Is Less Than* and then click **OK**.

Your worksheet now displays only the six employees in the Sales department who have a Rate below $14. Notice the Filter symbol displays beside the two columns with filters applied to them, Department and Rate.

8. The company decides to pay all Sales employees a minimum of $14 per hour, so adjust the Rate for the six employees to **14**.

9. Choose **Data→Sort & Filter→Filter** ▼ to remove all filters and redisplay all data.

10. Save the workbook.

Perform Advanced Calculations

There are many functions available in the Excel Function Library, but most of us use only a handful of these on a regular basis. Once you understand simple functions like SUM and AVERAGE, you can start exploring additional, more advanced functions. As you learn more about functions, it becomes easier to understand which functions to use and how to insert the function with the correct arguments.

The IF Function

Another fairly common function that can be quite useful is the IF Function. The IF function allows you to determine the value of a cell based on the outcome of a logical test. The IF function also provides the basis for many other formulas, such as COUNTIF and SUMIF. Although the IF function seems rather challenging at first, with some practice it becomes much easier, almost like forming a sentence in the form of a question.

The IF function is useful in situations in which there are two possible outcomes, and there are defined criteria to determine the outcome. For example, if you offer sales employees a $100 bonus if they achieve $5,000 in sales for the month, you can use an IF function to determine which employees qualify. In this case, $5,000 is the criterion, which needs to be written as a logical test.

 View the video "Using the IF Function."

THE IF FUNCTION

Arguments	Description	Examples
Logical Test	This is a question or criterion, which must be a yes/no, true/false question and which usually includes at least one cell reference.	D2>5000 D2>=A1
There are two possible outcomes, so you need to enter two values.		
Value if true	If the answer is true, this determines what result is placed in the cell after completing the formula. The result can be text, numbers, cell references, or even another formula.	100 "Yes" D2*10%
Value if false	If the answer is not true, it must be false, so what will the result be? Again, the result can be text, numbers, cell references, or a formula.	0 "No" D2*2%

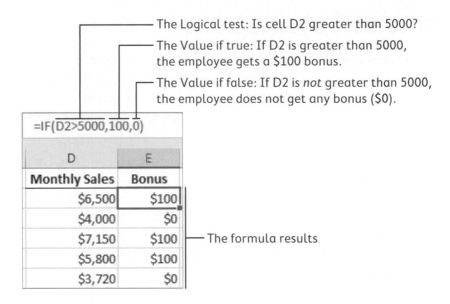

The Logical test: Is cell D2 greater than 5000?

The Value if true: If D2 is greater than 5000, the employee gets a $100 bonus.

The Value if false: If D2 is *not* greater than 5000, the employee does not get any bonus ($0).

=IF(D2>5000,100,0)

Monthly Sales	Bonus
$6,500	$100
$4,000	$0
$7,150	$100
$5,800	$100
$3,720	$0

The formula results

DEVELOP YOUR SKILLS: E4-D5

In this exercise, you will create several formulas using the IF function to calculate the number of regular hours and overtime hours each employee worked. You will then calculate total Gross Pay.

1. Save your workbook as **E4-D5-PayrollP17**.
2. Select **cell I6** and click **Insert Function** *fx* on the Formula Bar.
3. Choose the **IF** function (under the Logical category, if necessary) and then click **OK**.
4. Follow these steps to create a formula using the IF function to calculate the number of Regular Hours for employees:

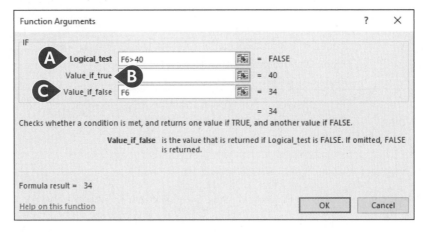

Ⓐ In the **Logical_Test** box enter **F6>40**, which will determine whether the employee worked more than 40 hours.

Ⓑ In the **Value_If_True** box enter **40**, because if the employee did in fact work more than 40 hours, that person would receive regular pay for 40 hours and the rest would be considered overtime.

Ⓒ In the **Value_If_False** box enter **F6**, because if the employee worked 40 hours or less, all of the hours worked would be considered regular hours. Then click **OK**.

The result of the formula is 34 because Jasmin worked 34 hours, so her Regular Hours equal 34.

5. Select **cell K6**, type the formula **=IF(F6>40,F6-40,0)**, and then complete the entry.

The Function arguments are typed inside brackets, separated by commas. The result of the formula is zero; Jasmin only worked 34 hours, so there are no Overtime Hours to be paid. To edit or to simply double-check the formula, you can click Insert Function to open the Function Arguments dialog box.

6. Click **Insert Function** fx and compare your screen to the following.

The Logical_test box has the same logical test, *F6>40*, which determines whether the employee worked more than 40 hours.

The Value_if_true box contains *F6-40*, because if the employee did in fact work more than 40 hours, that employee would receive overtime pay for the total number of hours less 40, the first 40 of which would be paid at the regular rate.

The Value_if_false box says 0, because if the employee worked 40 hours or less, that employee does not receive any overtime pay.

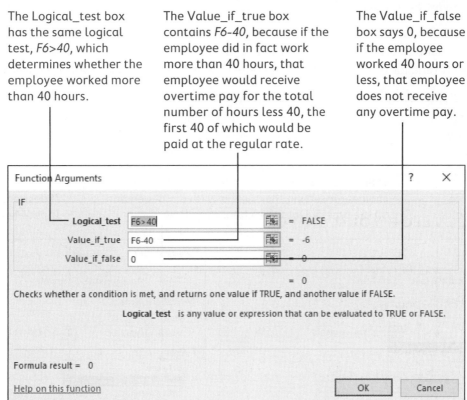

Function Arguments   ?   ✕

IF

Logical_test   F6>40   = FALSE

Value_if_true   F6-40   = -6

Value_if_false   0   = 0

= 0

Checks whether a condition is met, and returns one value if TRUE, and another value if FALSE.

     Logical_test is any value or expression that can be evaluated to TRUE or FALSE.

Formula result = 0

Help on this function   OK   Cancel

7. Click **OK** to close the window.

Since the Reg Hours and OT Hours have been calculated, you can now calculate Reg Pay and OT Pay for employees by multiplying hours by their rate.

8. Select **cell J6**, enter the formula **=I6*G6**, and then tap ⌗Tab⌗ twice.

9. In **cell L6** enter the formula **=K6*G6*1.5** and then tap ⌗Tab⌗ once.

We know that Jasmin doesn't receive any overtime, but you are setting up the formula to calculate OT Pay for all employees. OT Pay is OT Hours x Rate x 1.5 because employees get time and a half for overtime (100% + 50% = 150% or 1.5).

10. Enter the formula for Gross Pay, which is **=J6+L6+H6**, and complete the entry.

Total Gross Pay includes Reg Pay, OT Pay, and Commissions.

11. With **cell M6** active, choose **Home→Number→Number Format→Currency** and then choose **Home→Font→Bold**.

12. Select the **range I6:M6** and double-click the fill handle to fill down the formulas for all employees.

Double-clicking is much easier in this case than dragging the fill handle all the way down to row 62. The Gross Pay is now calculated for all of the employees. You can double-check your formulas visually by checking a few examples of employees who worked overtime and a few who didn't. For example, you can quickly see that Cam Owens in row 11 worked 47 hours and received 7 hours of OT Pay.

13. Save and close the workbook.

Controlling Data Entry with Data Validation

When entering values into an Excel worksheet, it is important to be consistent and accurate. However, mistakes can be made, especially if you ask someone else to do the data entry for you. To ensure accuracy and consistency, you can use data validation to create criteria for cells that limit the possible entries into those cells.

Normally you would set up data validation before entering the values because creating criteria for a cell that already contains data won't tell you if it has been correctly entered. You also need to create the criteria for all cells, so you would select the entire range where you intend to enter the data.

The criteria you choose can restrict the type of data as well as the range of acceptable values. For example, you could restrict data entry to whole numbers between 0 and 100, or you could restrict data entry to a text list. You can also create a custom Input Message to assist the user in entering the acceptable data and an Error Alert if they enter an unacceptable value.

First choose to allow Any Value.

Then set the desired criteria for the Data; the choices for setting the criteria will vary depending on the type of Data you choose to allow.

If desired, create an Input Message or Error Alert.

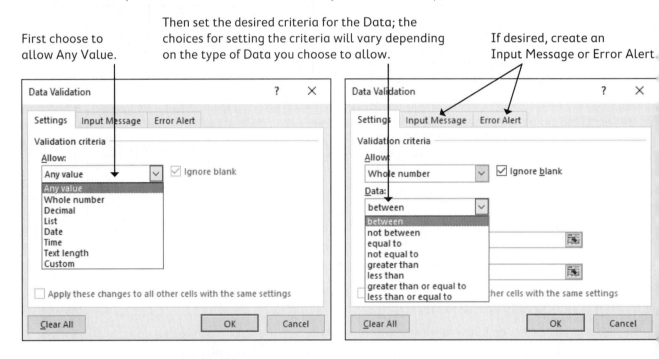

Data→Data Tools→Data Validation

DEVELOP YOUR SKILLS: E4-D6

In this exercise, you will create data validation criteria to choose the Department for each employee from a list and to restrict the number of hours that can be entered.

1. Open **E4-D6-Payroll** from the **Excel Chapter 4** folder and save it as **E4-D6-PayrollRevised**.

   You will be using data validation to ensure the Department is entered correctly, using one of three choices from a list.

2. Follow these steps to create the data validation rule:

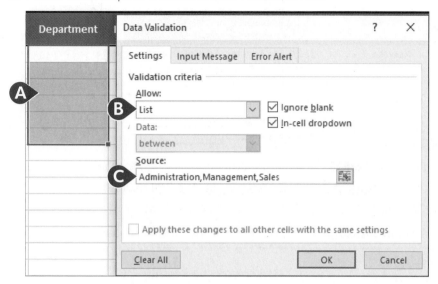

Ⓐ Select the cells where data will be entered, which is in the **range E6:E11**, and then choose **Data→Data Tools→Data Validation**.

Ⓑ Select **List** using the **Allow menu** button▼.

Allowing the List type of data means only the values you specify, which the user can choose from a List, can be entered into the cells.

Ⓒ In the **Source** box type `Administration,Management,Sales` separated by commas but no spaces and then click **OK**.

The three items typed into the Source box will appear for the user to choose from; an alternative to typing the source options is using cell references to a list of items on your worksheet.

3. Select **cell E6**.

4. Type `Admin` and then tap `Enter`.

A window will pop up telling you the value you entered doesn't match the data validation restrictions for the cell.

5. Click **Cancel**.

Notice the drop-down menu button ▼ to the right of the cell, which displays the options you typed for the source of the list.

6. Use the **menu** button ▼ to select **Administration** from the list of Departments for Jasmin in **cell E6**.

7. Insert the following Departments for the other five employees:

First Name	Last Name	Employee ID#	Location	Department	H
Jasmin	Newton	13651	Los Angeles	Administration	
Tim	Parker	17232	Los Angeles	Administration	
Carol	Gregory	16688	Los Angeles	Management	
Kobe	Curry	20303	Los Angeles	Sales	
Tracy	Bryant	14917	Los Angeles	Sales	
Cam	Owens	22404	Los Angeles	Sales	

8. Select the **range F6:F11** to create data validation criteria for the Hours to be entered.

9. Choose **Data→Data Tools→Data Validation** and then set the criteria to allow only a **Whole Number** between **0** (Minimum) and **60** (Maximum).

10. Click the **Input Message** tab and enter the **Input Message** as follows:

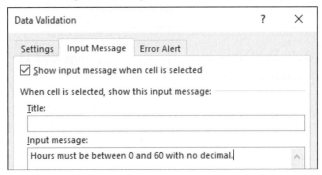

11. Click **OK** to complete the settings and then select **cell F6**.

   Notice a ScreenTip appears with the message you entered.

12. Test the data validation by typing **61** in **cell F6** and then tapping Enter. Read the message and then click **Retry**. Test it again by typing **40.5**, tap Enter, and then click **Cancel** to stop editing the cell.

   If you need someone else to enter the data, you can be confident no data will be entered that doesn't meet your criteria; for example, accidentally paying someone for 400 hours instead of 40!

13. Save and close the workbook.

Printing Options for Large Worksheets

To print large worksheets in a presentable format, you may need to make some adjustments to your worksheet. For example, you may want to ensure that column headings are visible on all pages, you may want to choose how your data is divided across several pages, or you may want to add additional information that isn't part of the worksheet itself to the top or bottom of each printed page.

PRINTING OPTIONS

Feature	Description
Print Titles	This option enables you to print the same headings on all pages by repeating either the same rows or the same columns on all pages.
Print Area	This option enables you to print only a specific area of your worksheet, rather than the whole thing.

PRINTING OPTIONS

Feature	Description
Breaks	This option enables you to determine where one page ends and the next page begins for printing purposes. Page breaks in Excel are both horizontal and vertical. Existing Page Breaks can be moved, or new ones can be inserted.
Scale to Fit	This option enables you to force your data onto a desired number of pages, using width and height, by scaling or shrinking the size of the worksheet contents.

 View the video "Printing a Large Worksheet."

≡ Page Layout→Page Setup

Add a Header or Footer

When you are printing a worksheet, you may want information included on the printout that doesn't need to be shown on the screen. This might include information such as a title, company name, your own name, the page number, or perhaps the date.

In Excel, both the Header and Footer have three sections. These are not part of the worksheet, so they do not have a cell address like the worksheet cells.

≡ Insert→Text→Header & Footer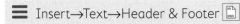

≡ View→Workbook Views→Page Layout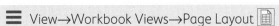

DEVELOP YOUR SKILLS: E4-D7

In this exercise, you will set up the Print Area, repeat the column headings, and adjust other print settings.

1. Open **E4-D5-PayrollP17** from your **Excel Chapter 4** folder and save it as **E4-D7-PayrollP17**.

2. Go to **File→Print** to view the Print Preview.

   Notice the worksheet prints on four pages, and the Gross Pay column is on pages three and four; the first adjustment to be made is to adjust the worksheet width to one page.

3. Use the **Back** button to go back to your worksheet.

4. Choose **Page Layout→Scale to Fit→Width→1 page**.

5. Go back to the **Print Preview** and see that the worksheet now prints on two pages; one page wide and two pages long.

Print Repeating Headings

6. Use the **Back** button to go back to your worksheet.

7. Choose **Page Layout→Page Setup→Print Titles** 🖨.

8. Follow these steps to print repeating headings:

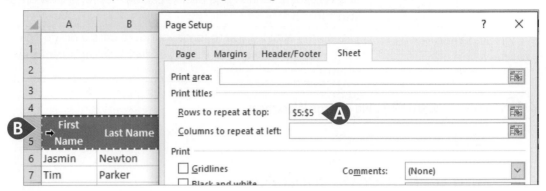

Ⓐ Select the box next to **Rows to Repeat at Top**.

Ⓑ Click anywhere in **row 5**.

By clicking to select the row, Excel will add the correct formatting to the row reference.

9. Click **OK**.

You won't notice anything different in the current view, but you can check the Print Preview to see the repeating row on page two.

10. Choose **File→Print** and below the Print Preview use the right-pointing arrow to advance to page two.

Now you can see the same headings with the blue background that are printed on page one.

11. Use the **Back** button to go back to your worksheet.

Set the Print Area

12. Select the **range A5:M11**.

You must select the desired range before setting the print area.

13. Choose **Page Layout→Page Setup→Print Area** 🖨**→Set Print Area**.

This means only the selected range will print, which is only the Los Angeles employees. You can check this by again going to Print Preview.

14. Go to **Print Preview** to view the change and then return to your worksheet.

15. Choose **Page Layout→Page Setup→Print Area** 🖨**→Clear Print Area**.

Now the whole worksheet will print once again because the specified print area has been cleared.

Set Page Breaks

16. Switch your view to **Page Break Preview**.

You can see there are two pages in the print area, and the page break falls between Sarah Mckinnon *and* Kristen Chambers. *Page Break Preview is the best view for adding/adjusting the page breaks.*

17. Place the mouse pointer over the Page Break line to display the two-way arrow as shown below and then drag the **Page Break** up to below **row 11**, where the data for Los Angeles employees ends and Miami begins.

32	Jaime	Burgess	16340	Ne
33	Shaq	McGrady	15695	Ne
34	Sara	Mckinnon	13041	Ne
35	Kristen	Chambers	17641	Ne
36	Terrence	King	14767	Ne
37	Lorraine	Martine	12731	Ne

Because the area below the page break is too big to fit on one page, Excel automatically adds a new Page Break, so your worksheet will now print on three pages.

18. Drag the new **Page Break** up below **row 28**, where the data for Miami employees ends.

19. Excel inserts another new Page Break, so drag the new **Page Break** up below **row 37**, where the data for New York employees ends.

Because the rest of the data does fit on one page, you have to manually insert another Page Break yourself to put Toronto and Vancouver on separate pages.

20. Select **cell A52** and then choose **Page Layout→Page Setup→Breaks** ⊞ **→Insert Page Break**.

21. Switch the view back to **Normal** and go to the **Print Preview**.

Notice that the data will print on five pages, one for each location, with the column headings repeated at the top of each page.

Insert Header

22. Return to your worksheet and then change the view to **Page Layout** and select the left header section.

You will see the Header & Footer Tools Design tab appears on the Ribbon, which allows you to insert formatted elements like Page Number and Current Date.

23. Choose **Header & Footer Tools Design→Header & Footer Elements→File Name** 🗋.

Notice there is a code that is inserted, but the code will display and print the File Name; if the File Name ever changes, it updates automatically.

24. Insert the **Page Number** 🗋 in the center Header section.

25. Insert the **Current Date** 🗓 in the right Header section.

26. Click on the worksheet outside of the header area, switch the view back to **Normal**, and then go to the **Print Preview** one last time.

Your Print Preview should look like this for page one.

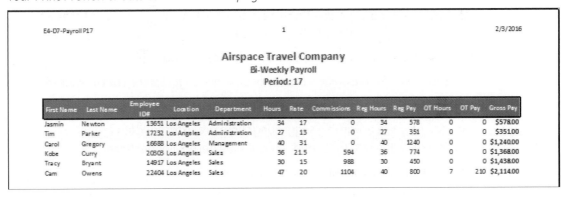

26. Save the workbook.

Create Tables

Tables allow you to more easily organize and analyze related data. Tables simplify the process of performing sorts, filtering your data, calculating totals, and even modifying the format of your data. The process of taking existing data and inserting a table is very simple, and you can convert a table back to a normal range of cells at any time without losing any data.

The Header Row makes sort and filter easy to access via the menu button ▼ in the header cell.

Banded Rows (alternating colors) can be added or removed, and you can modify colors with Table Styles.

Employee Name	Department	Salary
Carol Gregory	Sales	$40,000
Natasha Dyas	Admin.	$34,500
James Norman	Management	$68,000
Joshua Garcia	Sales	$46,000
Sarah Mckinnon	Sales	$42,750
Shannon Miller	Management	$52,000
Katrina Kormylo	Admin.	$48,000
Susan Colley	Sales	$44,800
William Emerson	Admin.	$41,000
Eugene Fink	Sales	$37,000

Employee Name ▼	Department ▼	Salary ▼
Carol Gregory	Sales	$40,000
Natasha Dyas	Admin.	$34,500
James Norman	Management	$68,000
Joshua Garcia	Sales	$46,000
Sarah Mckinnon	Sales	$42,750
Shannon Miller	Management	$52,000
Katrina Kormylo	Admin.	$48,000
Susan Colley	Sales	$44,800
William Emerson	Admin.	$41,000
Eugene Fink	Sales	$37,000
Total	10	$454,050

The Total Row makes it easy to add functions like Count (Department) and Sum (Salary) via the cell menu button ▼.

The same data, before and after a table is inserted

As you add more data at the bottom or right of the table, the table area expands to include the new adjacent rows or columns. Another nice feature is that entering a formula in one table cell will automatically copy the formula to all cells in that table column.

≡ Insert→Tables→Table 🗔

≡ Table Tools→Design→Tools→Convert to Range

DEVELOP YOUR SKILLS: E4-D8

In this exercise, you will create a table and use the table features to perform tasks like filter, sort, and calculate totals.

1. Save your file as **E4-D8-PayrollP17**.
2. Select **cell J6** and choose **Insert→Tables→Table** 🗔.

   *Excel looks for the adjacent range of data and suggests the **range A5:M63**, with table headers.*
3. Click **OK** to accept the suggested table area.
4. You may see a warning suggesting there are external data ranges. If you do, click **Yes** to convert the selection to a table and remove all external connections.
5. Click the **Department menu** button ▼.

   Notice the sort and filtering options available.

6. Uncheck the filter boxes for **Administration** and **Sales** and click **OK**.

   Only employees in the Management department are now visible in the list.

7. Use the **Rate menu** button ▼ to sort the Management department employees by Rate, from highest to lowest.

8. Choose **Table Tools→Design→Table Style Options→Total Row** to add a total at the bottom of the table.

   Notice that in the cell directly below Gross Pay there is a total automatically calculated for the Management department.

9. Select **cell F64**, click the **menu** button ▼, and select **Sum**.

   The total hours for Management employees is calculated, showing 416 hours.

10. Change the Table Style to **Medium 1**.

11. Use the **Department** filter to clear Management and display the **Sales** department only.

12. Use the **Location menu** button ▼ to re-sort the data by **Location** from **A to Z**.

    Locations should be listed in order from A to Z, and the Total row at the bottom of the table should recalculate the total Hours and Gross Pay as follows.

First Name ▼	Hours ▼	Gross Pay ▼
Total	1152	$40,921.50

13. Save the workbook and close Excel.

Self-Assessment

Check your knowledge of this chapter's key concepts and skills using the Self-Assessment in your ebook or eLab course.

Reinforce Your Skills

Import and Organize Data for a Donor List

In this exercise, you will open a template, import data from the Kids for Change donors this year, and then organize the data appropriately.

1. Open the **E4-R1-DonorList** template from the **Excel Chapter 4** folder.
2. Use **Save As** to save the document and replace the *1* at the end of the filename with the current year.

   The donor information is saved in a CSV file, so you need to import it into the current workbook.
3. Select **cell A4** and choose **Data→Get External Data→From Text** 🔲.
4. Navigate to the **E4-R1-DonorData** CSV file in the **Excel Chapter 4** folder and click **Import**.
5. Use the Text Import Wizard to import the data, ensuring you select the comma delimiter in step 2 and import the data into **cell A4**.
6. Adjust column widths as necessary so the headings display properly.
7. If necessary, select **cell A4** again and **Freeze Panes**.
8. Scroll down to ensure the data was imported correctly. *Nicki Hollinger* should be the last donor on the list in **row 45**.
9. Scroll to the top of your data and then sort the data with a multiple-level sort, first by **Donor Type**, **A to Z**, and then by **First Donation**, **Oldest to Newest**.
10. Filter your data to display only the Donors with Total Annual Donations greater than 5,000.

    These are your high-priority donors; you want them to stand out in the list, so you will add a Fill Color to these rows.
11. With the data still filtered, select the range of cells that contains the donor data and include the blank column below *Free Membership*.
12. Apply Fill Color **Green, Accent 6, Lighter 40%**.
13. Remove the filter from the data.
14. Save the workbook.

Use the IF Function

In this exercise, you will add information about the Kids for Change donors, using the IF function and data validation, and adjust the sheet for printing.

1. Save your workbook as **E4-R2-DonorList2016**.
2. Insert a new column to the left of *Phone #* and type **Contact OK** in **cell C3** for the new heading.

   It is important to ensure you have permission before calling your donors, so you will list Yes or No for each donor.
3. Select all cells in **column C** below the heading *Contact OK* in the **range C4:C45**.

4. Create a data validation rule using a List, which will allow users to enter only the text *Yes* or *No*.

   All but two donors have given you permission to contact them, so you can fill in this information for all donors now. (Hint: It will be quicker to use the Fill Handle to fill in "Yes" for everyone first and then adjust the entry to "No" for the other two donors.)

5. Enter **Yes** in the Contact OK column for all donors. (Hint: If you use the Fill Handle, use the AutoFill Options to adjust to Fill Without Formatting.)

6. Scroll through the list and change the entry to **No** for Eastjet and Crystal Robinson (rows 14 and 23).

   A local business is offering free memberships to donors with Total Annual Donations greater than $7,500, so you will create a formula to determine which donors qualify for a free membership.

7. Select **cell G4** and enter a formula using the **IF** function and the following arguments.

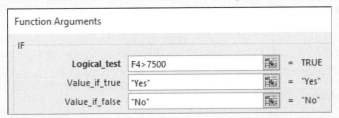

8. Copy the formula down the column using **AutoFill** and adjust the option to **Fill Without Formatting**.

9. **Center align** the **range G4:G45** with the IF function you just entered.

10. Go to the **Page Break Preview**.

11. To adjust the list to fit nicely onto two pages, adjust the Page Break to fall between *Business* and *Private* in the Donor Type column.

12. Return to **Normal** view and set up the page layout to repeat **rows 1:3** at the top of each page.

13. Select **cell A3** and insert a table using your data in the **range A3:G45**; check off **My Table Has Headers**, if necessary.

    Inserting a table affects the column width, so you need to readjust the column width and Page Layout options.

14. Adjust the widths of **columns F** and **G** to **13** and then use **Scale to Fit** to ensure the page **Width** is **1 Page**.

15. Use the **Table Tools** remove the **Banded Rows**.

16. Add a **Total Row** to the bottom of the table.

17. In the **Total Row** add the **Sum** to the Total Annual Donation column, and in the Free Membership column remove the **Count** function. (Hint: To remove a function, click the **menu** button ▼ and choose **None**.)

18. Apply the **Currency** number format, with no decimals, to the **Total**.

19. Save the workbook and close Excel.

Organize a Large Worksheet and Use the IF Function

In this exercise, you will the import information about students who have volunteered for Kids for Change this quarter and use the skills learned in this chapter.

1. Open **E4-R3-StudentHours** from your **Excel Chapter 4** folder and save it as `E4-R3-StudentHoursRevised`.

2. Import the data in the CSV file **E4-R3-StudentData** from the **Excel Chapter 4** folder into **cell A4**.

3. Adjust the column width for **columns D:F** to **7**.

4. In **column G**, insert the heading `Total` and then use **AutoSum** to calculate the total for each student.

   Students who volunteer 60 hours or more are invited to an appreciation dinner each quarter, so you will use an IF formula to determine who is invited.

5. In **cell H3** enter `Dinner Invite` for the heading.

6. Create an **IF** function in **cell H4**, which will insert *Yes* for students with 60 or more hours and *No* for those who have fewer than 60.

7. **Center Align** and **Bold** the result in **cell H4** and then fill the formula down the column for the other students.

8. Now **Freeze** the panes so the top three rows remain visible at all times.

9. Perform a multiple level sort on your data, so the students are listed from A to Z by school and then by total from largest to smallest.

10. Next create a table from your data that includes the **range A3:H26**.

11. Now **Filter** your table to include only students who have *Yes* in the Dinner Invite column.

12. Adjust the page layout orientation to **Landscape** and then insert a **Page Break** below each of the first three schools, so each school prints on a separate page.

13. Save the workbook and close Excel.

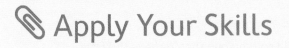# Apply Your Skills

APPLY YOUR SKILLS: E4-A1

Import and Sort Data

In this exercise, you will import the expenses for Universal Corporate events into a template so that you can organize the data.

1. Start Excel, open the **E4-A1-Expenses** template file from your **Excel Chapter 4** folder, and save it as **E4-A1-ExpensesQ3**.

2. Insert a column in **column C** and enter the heading **Budget**.

3. Import the data for Q3 from the **E4-A1-ExpData** CSV file located in your **Excel Chapter 4** folder into **cell A6**.

4. Adjust the width of **columns C:F** to **11**.

5. Freeze all rows above **row 6**.

6. Sort your data by **Category** and then by **Expense**, both **A to Z**.

   Auto Repairs should now be in row 6.

7. Add a total in **column G** with an appropriate heading that calculates the three-month total for each type of expense.

   Be sure not to include the budget amount in the total.

8. Apply the **Accounting** format to the total in **column G**, with no decimals.

9. Copy the formula down the column for all expenses.

10. Save the workbook.

APPLY YOUR SKILLS: E4-A2

Use Tables and the IF Function

In this exercise, you will determine if Universal Corporate Events went over budget on each of the expense items.

1. Save your workbook as **E4-A2-ExpensesQ3**.

   To identify which Expenses were over budget, you will use the IF Function in a formula.

2. In **cell H5** enter the heading **O/U**.

3. In **cell H6** enter the following formula: **=IF(G6>C6,"OVER","Under")**.

   This formula compares the Total to the Budget amount and returns the text Under or OVER (in caps).

4. Copy the formula down the column for all expenses. (Hint: You can ignore the error that appears.)

5. Insert a **Table** using all of the data in the **range A5:H46**.

6. Remove the Banded Rows formatting.

7. Insert a **Total Row** and add a **Sum** at the bottom of the data for all five columns with numerical data: *Budget, July, August, September,* and *Total.*

8. Remove the Total from the O/U column.

9. Filter the table to display only the Expenses that were OVER budget.

10. Apply a **light gold fill** and **Bold** to the O/U column and then remove the filter.

11. Select the **range A1:H10** and set the **Print Area** so that only the Auto expenses will print.

12. Save the workbook and close Excel.

APPLY YOUR SKILLS: E4-A3

Organize a Large Worksheet and Use Data Validation

In this exercise, you will import data that Universal Corporate Events collected from its clients over the past two months so you can organize and analyze the data.

1. Start Excel, open **E4-A3-Feedback** from the **Excel Chapter 4** folder, and save it as **E4-A3-FeedbackRevised**.

2. Import the data from the **E4-A3-FBData** CSV file located in your **Excel Chapter 4** folder.

3. Adjust the column widths in which data was imported, as necessary.

4. Create a formula in **cell H5** to calculate the average rating from each customer based on the three surveys.

5. Copy the formula down the column for all clients and edit the number format to show only one decimal.

6. **Freeze Panes** so that **rows 1:4** are always showing.

7. **Sort** your data by **Event (A to Z)** and then by **Average Rating (Largest to Smallest)**.

8. Identify anyone who gave you an average rating above 6.0 by creating an **IF** function in **cell I5** to insert **YES** for those above 6.0 and **NO** for those at or below 6.0.

9. Copy the formula down the column for all clients and **Center** the data in that column.

10. Offer a coupon to those who were below 6.0 and found their event unsatisfactory, but also enter a data validation rule to prevent the coupon amount from exceeding $200.

11. Select the range below *Coupon Offered* for all clients and create a data validation rule that only allows whole numbers between **0** and **200**.

12. Enter the coupon amounts. Start by entering **$0** for all clients and then editing the coupon amount for clients NOT above 6.0 as follows: Stormy BBQ gets **$100** and Wilson Samuels Corp. gets **$200**.

13. Go to the **Page Break Preview** and insert **Page Breaks** between *Staff Party Events* and *Team Building Events*, and *Team Building Events* and *Training Events*.

14. Use **Print Titles** to repeat **row 4** at the top of each page.

15. Go to **Page Layout** view and insert the **Current Date** in the left footer section and the **Page Number** in the right footer section.

16. Return to **Normal** view.

    If you like, check your work in Print Preview to see if it will print properly—on three pages with the titles at the top and the footers at the bottom of each page.

17. Save the workbook and close Excel.

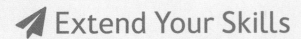 Extend Your Skills

These exercises challenge you to think critically and apply your new skills. You will be evaluated on your ability to follow directions, completeness, creativity, and the use of proper grammar and mechanics. Save files to your chapter folder. Submit assignments as directed.

E4-E1   That's the Way I See It

A friend of yours is teaching a course at Learn Fast College for the first time. She knows you are an Excel expert and needs your help getting her grades from a CSV file into an Excel file with the appropriate formatting. Start with a blank workbook and import the data from the **E4-E1-GradesData** CSV file, leaving some room at the top to add titles later. Save your file as **E4-E1-Grades**. Format the headings appropriately and adjust column width as needed. Create a data validation rule so that participation grades must be between 0 and 10, which will be entered by her later. Then use a formula to specify which students qualify for the attendance award; to qualify, their attendance must be perfect. Lastly, sort the data by Status and Student ID and make any other adjustments that would make it easier for your friend to print the worksheet, if desired. Save the workbook.

E4-E2   Be Your Own Boss

At the end of the year, you always add up all of the hours that the clients of your business, Blue Jean Landscaping, put into their own landscaping work. You have a template created in a prior year, **E4-E2-ClientHours**. You need to open the template and import the data for this year from the file **E4-E2-ClientData**, which is a CSV file located in the same folder. Once you have done this, save the file as **E4-E2-ClientHoursRevised**. You need to find the total for each client and sort the data by Customer Type and then by Total. Then use the IF function to create a formula in a new column, where the customers with more than 100 hours get a discount of $17/hour, and the customers with fewer than 100 hours get $15/hour. Ensure that the maximum number of hours that can be entered per month is 40 and use the data validation tools to circle invalid data. Correct any numbers entered that are greater than 40 to be 40. Create a table with your data so that you can insert a total row at the bottom for all months. Make any other adjustments that would make it easier to print the worksheet if desired. Save the workbook.

E4-E3   Demonstrate Proficiency

Stormy BBQ has an inventory list of ingredients from the kitchen, with the amount of stock for each item as well as the required amount. The data is in the file **E4-E3-KitSupplies** in CSV format. The data needs to be imported to an Excel file to organize it and to use the information to determine whether the item needs to be reordered. After you have imported the data into a new workbook, save the workbook as **E4-E3-KitSuppliesRevised**, insert titles, and apply formatting as you see fit. Then in the order column use a formula to determine if the item needs to be ordered. (Hint: If the In Stock number is less than the Requ'd Amt number, enter **YES** in the Order column.) Organize your list by sorting in an appropriate manner and then prepare the file for printing, if necessary. Save the workbook.

Glossary

adjacent Arrangement of cells, objects, or files that are next to each other; may be selected as a group by using Shift; also known as *contiguous*

alignment Horizontal placement of text relative to the left and right margins of a cell or a page, where text is left-, right-, or center-aligned; or vertical placement of text relative to the top and bottom margins of a cell or page, where text is top-, middle-, or bottom-aligned

argument The information or values, such as numbers, text, or cell references, used by a function in Excel to solve a formula

AutoComplete A feature that offers to complete the typing for you when it recognizes certain words or phrases

AutoFill A feature that extends a series, copies data, or copies a formula into adjacent cells

cell(s) A box formed by the intersection of a row and column in a worksheet or table, in which information is entered and displayed

cell references Sets of coordinates that indicate the location of a cells on a worksheet; for example, the cell reference D2 indicates a cell that appears at the intersection of column D and row 2

citation A reference to a source used in a document; contains information to locate the source

conditional formatting Formatting that is applied to cell contents only when user-specified criteria are met

contextual tab(s) Hidden Ribbon tabs that only appear when certain types of objects, such as pictures or tables, are selected

CSV Interchangeable file format where values such as text and numbers are separated by commas

data validation Feature used to limit the type of data and values that are allowed to be entered in a cell and to provide the user with messages to guide them when entering data

database A collection of data related to a particular subject or purpose, organized by records and fields; for example, an employee database contains information for each employee, such as their name, employee ID, and contact information

default Setting or name that a computer program uses until you specify otherwise

delimiter A character such as a comma, space, or tab that is used to specify a boundary between fields in data files

dragging (drag) Clicking and holding down the left mouse button while moving the mouse pointer; used for many tasks such as selecting, moving, and resizing text, objects, cells, columns, or rows

field A group or category of specific information or data, such as last names or phone numbers

filtering (filter) Process used to display only the rows of data that meet the conditions specified

formula A cell entry that uses a sequence of values, cell references, names, functions, or operators to perform a mathematical calculation and produce a new value; always begins with an equal sign (=)

Formula Bar A bar above the Excel worksheet that can be used to enter or edit values or formulas in cells; displays the constant value or formula stored in the active cell

Freeze To set a row or column so that it remains visible at the top or left of the screen while scrolling

function A specific formula that takes an input value or values in the form of arguments, performs an operation, and returns a value or values; functions simplify the creation of formulas and are useful for lengthy or complex calculations

link Objects and formulas can be linked to connect the information from the source to the destination; the source can be on the same sheet, another sheet, or another workbook, and the destination is updated when the source is modified

name A word or string of characters that is created or defined to represent a cell or range of cells, which can then be used for navigation or used as a cell reference in a formula

Name Box Box on the left side of the Formula Bar that identifies the selected cell; can also be used for navigating to another cell or creating a new name for the selected cell

nonadjacent The arrangement of cells, objects, or files not next to each other; may be selected as a group using Ctrl; also known as *noncontiguous*

Ribbon Band at the top of an application window that contains the commands required to complete a task; organized in tabs that relate to a particular type of activity and groups of related commands (some tabs are only shown when needed, such as Chart Tools, Table Tools, or Picture Tools)

Scale to Fit (Scale) Process that increases or reduces size to a percentage of its original size; can be applied to an object or to a worksheet for printing

sort Process used to arrange data in a specific order, such as alphabetic, numeric, by date, or in ascending or descending order

tab Area on the Ribbon that displays an organized collection of commands; some tabs are only shown when needed, such as Chart Tools, Table Tools, or Picture Tools OR a keyboard key used to complete a cell entry and move one cell to the right

table A related collection of data about a particular subject that is stored in records (rows) and fields (columns) that allow for easier sorting, filtering, formatting, and calculations using structured references

template A preformatted document or workbook layout used as the basis for new documents to maintain consistency among documents and save the user time and that usually contains text, paragraph, table, graphical, and other types of formatting; in Excel, can also include formulas

workbook A collection of one or more worksheets saved together as one file

worksheet A collection of information, or blank space to enter new information, divided into columns and rows that form cells

Index

Note: Index entries ending in "V" indicate that a term is discussed in the video referenced on that page.